Fiction and Poetry

Key Stage 2

Years 5 and 6
Scotland P6-P7

Wendy Wren

First published in 2000 by:
Stanley Thornes (Publishers) Ltd

Reprinted in 2001 by:
Nelson Thornes Ltd
Delta Place
27 Bath Road
CHELTENHAM
GL53 7TH
United Kingdom

01 02 03 04 05 / 10 9 8 7 6 5 4 3 2

A catalogue record of this book is available from the British Library

ISBN 0 7487 4375 8

Illustrations by Vali Herzer
Page make-up by Tech-Set Ltd.

Printed and bound in Great Britain by The Bath Press, Bath

**Nelson Thornes publishes a comprehensive range of teacher resource books in the *Blueprints* and *Learning Targets* series. These titles provide busy teachers with unbeatable curriculum coverage, inspiration and value for money. For a complete list, please call our Primary Customer Services on 01242 267280, send an e-mail to cservice@nelsonthornes.com or write to:
Nelson Thornes Ltd, Freepost, Primary Customer Services, Delta Place, 27 Bath Road, Cheltenham GL53 7ZZ.
All Nelson Thornes titles can be bought by phone using a credit or debit card on 01242 267280 or online by visiting our website – www.nelsonthornes.com**

CONTENTS

Welcome to
LEARNING TARGETS

Learning Targets is a series of practical teacher's resource books written to help you to plan and deliver well-structured, professional lessons in line with all the relevant curriculum documents.

Each Learning Target book provides exceptionally clear lesson plans that cover the whole of its stated curriculum plus a large bank of carefully structured copymasters. Links to the key curriculum documents are provided throughout to enable you to plan effectively.

The Learning Targets series has been written in response to the challenge confronting teachers not just to come up with teaching ideas which cover the curriculum but to ensure that they deliver high quality lessons every lesson with the emphasis on raising standards of pupil achievement.

The recent thinking from OFSTED, and the National Literacy and Numeracy Strategies on the key factors in effective teaching has been built into the structure of Learning Targets. These might briefly be summarised as follows:

➤➤ that effective teaching is active teaching directed to very clear objectives

➤➤ that good lessons are delivered with pace, rigour and purpose

➤➤ that good teaching requires a range of strategies - including interactive whole class sessions

➤➤ that ongoing formative assessment is essential to plan children's learning

➤➤ that differentiation is necessary but that it must be realistic.

The emphasis in Learning Targets is on absolute clarity. We have written and designed the books to enable you to access and deliver effective lessons as easily as possible, with the following aims:

➤➤ to plan and deliver rigorous, well-structured lessons

➤➤ to set explicit targets for achievement in every lesson that you teach

➤➤ to make the children aware of what they are going to learn

➤➤ to put the emphasis on direct, active teaching every time

➤➤ to make effective use of time and resources

➤➤ to employ the full range of recommended strategies: whole-class, group and individual work

➤➤ to differentiate for ability groups realistically

➤➤ to use ongoing formative assessment to plan your next step

➤➤ to have ready access to usable pupil copymasters to support your teaching.

The page opposite provides an at-a-glance guide to the key features of the Learning Targets lessons and explains how they will enable you deliver effective lessons.
The key to symbols on the lesson plans is set out here. ➤➤

How to deliver structured lessons with pace, rigour and purpose

Explicit targets for achievement in every lesson

Concise advice on preparation

Crystal clear lesson plan layouts

The full range of teaching strategies

Rigorous and practical activities

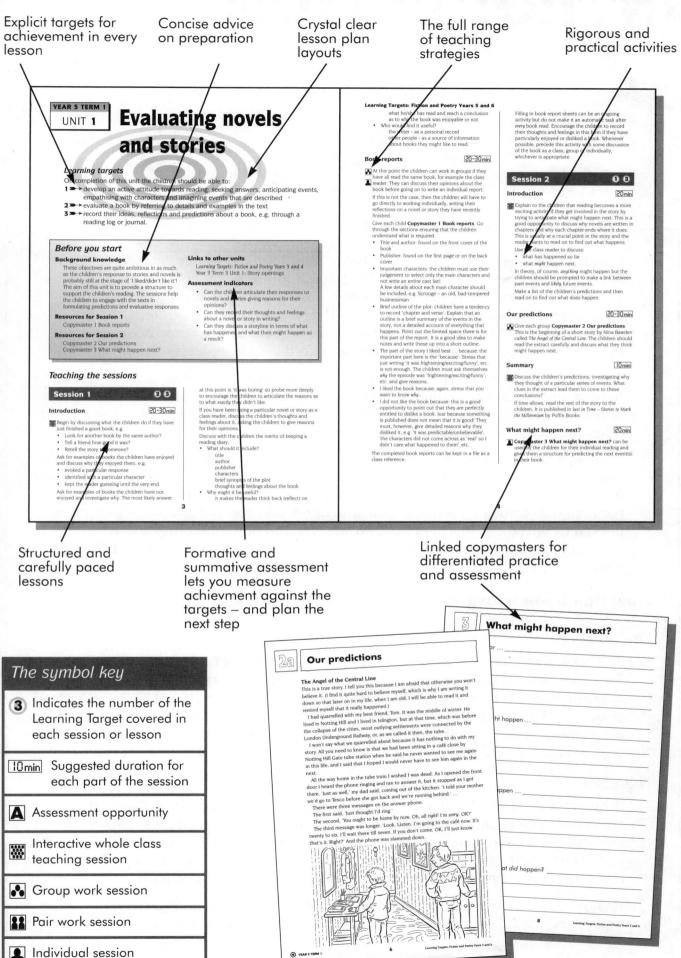

YEAR 5 TERM 1
UNIT 1

Evaluating novels and stories

Learning targets
On completion of this unit the children should be able to:
1 ➤ develop an active attitude towards reading: seeking answers, anticipating events, empathising with characters and imagining events that are described
2 ➤ evaluate a book by referring to details and examples in the text
3 ➤ record their ideas, reflections and predictions about a book, e.g. through a reading log or journal.

Before you start
Background knowledge
These objectives are quite ambitious in as much as the children's response to stories and novels is probably still at the stage of 'I liked/didn't like it'! The aim of this unit is to provide a structure to support the children's reading. The sessions help the children to engage with the texts in formulating predictions and evaluative responses.

Resources for Session 1
Copymaster 1 Book reports

Resources for Session 2
Copymaster 2 Our predictions
Copymaster 3 What might happen next?

Links to other units
Learning Targets: Fiction and Poetry Years 3 and 4
Year 3 Term 3 Unit 1: Story openings

Assessment indicators
• Can the children articulate their responses to novels and stories giving reasons for their opinions?
• Can they record their thoughts and feelings about a novel or story in writing?
• Can they discuss a storyline in terms of what has happened and what then might happen as a result?

Teaching the sessions

Session 1   2 3

Introduction   20–30min

Begin by discussing what the children do if they have just finished a good book, e.g.
• Look for another book by the same author?
• Tell a friend how good it was?
• Retell the story to someone?
Ask for examples of books the children have enjoyed and discuss why they enjoyed them, e.g.
• evoked a particular response
• identified with a particular character
• kept the reader guessing until the very end.
Ask for examples of books the children have not enjoyed and investigate why. The most likely answer

at this point is 'it was boring' so probe more deeply to encourage the children to articulate the reasons as to what exactly they didn't like.
If you have been using a particular novel or story as a class reader, discuss the children's thoughts and feelings about it, asking the children to give reasons for their opinions.
Discuss with the children the merits of keeping a reading diary:
• What should it include?
  title
  author
  publisher
  characters
  brief synopsis of the plot
  thoughts and feelings about the book
• Why might it be useful?
  it makes the reader think back (reflect) on

Learning Targets: Fiction and Poetry Years 5 and 6

what he/she has read and reach a conclusion as to why the book was enjoyable or not
• Who would find it useful?
  the writer - as a personal record
  other people - as a source of information about books they might like to read.

Book reports   20–30min

At this point the children can work in groups if they have all read the same book, for example the class reader. They can discuss their opinions about the book before going on to write an individual report.
If this is not the case, then the children will have to go directly to working individually, writing their reflections on a novel or story they have recently finished.
Give each child **Copymaster 1 Book reports**. Go through the sections ensuring that the children understand what is required.
• Title and author: found on the front cover of the book
• Publisher: found on the first page or on the back cover
• Important characters: the children must use their judgement to select only the main characters and not write an entire cast list!
A few details about each main character should be included, e.g. Scrooge – an old, bad-tempered businessman
• Brief outline of the plot: children have a tendency to record 'chapter and verse'. Explain that an outline is a brief summary of the events in the story, not a detailed account of everything that happens. Point out the limited space there is for this part of the report. It is a good idea to make notes and write these up into a short outline.
• The part of the story I liked best ... because: the important part here is the 'because'. Stress that just writing 'it was frightening/exciting/funny', etc. is not enough. The children must ask themselves why the episode was 'frightening/exciting/funny', etc. and give reasons.
• I liked the book because: again, stress that you want to know why.
• I did not like the book because: this is a good opportunity to point out that they are perfectly entitled to dislike a book. Just because something is published does not mean that it is good! They must, however, give detailed reasons why they disliked it, e.g. 'It was predictable/unbelievable', 'the characters did not come across as 'real' so I didn't care what happened to them', etc.

The completed book reports can be kept in a file as a class reference.

Filling in book report sheets can be an ongoing activity but do not make it an automatic task after every book read. Encourage the children to record their thoughts and feelings in this form if they have particularly enjoyed or disliked a book. Whenever possible, precede this activity with some discussion of the book as a class, group or individually, whichever is appropriate.

Session 2   1 3

Introduction   20min

Explain to the children that reading becomes a more exciting activity if they get involved in the story by trying to anticipate what might happen next. This is a good opportunity to discuss why novels are written in chapters and why each chapter ends where it does. This is usually at a crucial point in the story and the reader wants to read on to find out what happens.
Use the class reader to discuss:
• what has happened so far
• what might happen next.
In theory, of course, anything might happen but the children should be prompted to make a link between past events and likely future events.
Make a list of the children's predictions and then read on to find out what does happen.

Our predictions   20–30min

Give each group **Copymaster 2 Our predictions**. This is the beginning of a short story by Nina Bawden called The Angel of the Central Line. The children should read the extract carefully and discuss what they think might happen next.

Summary   10min

Discuss the children's predictions, investigating why they thought of a particular series of events. What clues in the extract lead them to come to these conclusions?
If time allows, read the rest of the story to the children. It is published in Just in Time – Stories to Mark the Millennium by Puffin Books.

What might happen next?   20min

Copymaster 3 What might happen next? can be used by the children for their individual reading and gives them a structure for predicting the next event(s) in their book.

3   4

Structured and carefully paced lessons

Formative and summative assessment lets you measure achievment against the targets – and plan the next step

Linked copymasters for differentiated practice and assessment

The symbol key

3	Indicates the number of the Learning Target covered in each session or lesson
10min	Suggested duration for each part of the session
A	Assessment opportunity
🖲	Interactive whole class teaching session
⚙	Group work session
👥	Pair work session
👤	Individual session

2a **Our predictions**

The Angel of the Central Line
This is a true story. I tell you this because I am afraid that otherwise you won't believe it. (I find it quite hard to believe myself, which is why I am writing it down so that later on in my life, when I am old, I will be able to read it and remind myself that it really happened.)
I had quarrelled with my best friend, Tom. It was the middle of winter. He lived in Notting Hill and I lived in Islington, but at that time, which was before the collapse of the cities, most outlying settlements were connected by the London Underground Railway, or, as we called it then, the tube.
I won't say what we quarrelled about because it has nothing to do with my story. All you need to know is that we had been sitting in a café close by Notting Hill Gate tube station when he said he never wanted to see me again in this life, and I said that I hoped I would never have to see him again in the next.
All the way home in the tube train I wished I was dead. As I opened the front door I heard the phone ringing and ran to answer it, but it stopped as I got there. 'Just as well,' my dad said, coming out of the kitchen. 'I told your mother we'd go to Tesco before she got back and we're running behind.' ...
There were three messages on the answer phone.
The first said, 'Just thought I'd ring.'
The second, 'You ought to be home by now. Oh, all right! I'm sorry. OK?'
The third message was longer. 'Look. Listen. I'm going to the café now. It's twenty to six. I'll wait there till seven. If you don't come, OK, I'll just know that's it. Right?' And the phone was slammed down.

YEAR 5 TERM 1   6   Learning Targets: Fiction and Poetry Years 5 and 6

3 **What might happen next?**

...ar ...

...ht happen ...

...ppen ...

...at did happen?

8   Learning Targets: Fiction and Poetry Years 5 and 6

v

INTRODUCTION

Learning Targets for Literacy: Fiction and Poetry Years 5 and 6 provides detailed coverage of comprehension and composition level work for English for fiction and poetry. Together with the accompanying book *Non-Fiction Years 5 and 6*, it provides an invaluable resource for text level work for the National Literacy Strategy and for Scotland P6–P7. The two other Learning Targets books at Key Stage 2, *Grammar and Punctuation* and *Spelling*, cover sentence and word level work respectively.

This book covers reading and writing fiction and poetry at the level of the text: how to read, understand and write all the relevant genres at Years 5 and 6. All the related decoding, spelling, handwriting and grammar skills for Key Stage 2 are covered in the other two books at this level.

This book is not, of course, a complete literacy scheme. It cannot provide you with all the resources needed to deliver text level literacy for fiction and poetry to your class. It is, however, a highly comprehensive resource book that covers all the main requirements through a series of well structured, detailed and specific lesson plans backed by linked copymasters that provide you with both pupil sheets and photocopiable materials that give you the reading materials you need to deliver the lessons.

How this book is organised

The sections

The book is divided into six sections. Each one covers one term's work in Years 5 and 6 for the National Literacy Strategy and closely follows the range of work and the detailed plans for fiction and poetry on pages 44–55 of the National Literacy Strategy document. Each section begins with a short overview of the term's work and provides assessment objectives linked to copymasters. A National Literacy Strategy planner is also included at this point.

The units

Sections are sub-divided into units. Each unit is an integrated piece of work that combines reading and writing skills to meet particular learning targets. These learning targets state explicitly what the children should aim to know or be able to do by the end of the unit and provide you with a set of clear, assessable objectives to teach any lesson on reading and writing fiction and poetry at text level.

Together, the units in a section form an overall set of lesson plans to cover the term's work. They are 'free-standing' so that in Section 1 Year 5 Term 1 you can, for example, use Unit 2 on portraying characters to meet a particular objective within your teaching programme without having undertaken Unit 1 on evaluating novels and stories. In general, units at the beginning of a section are easier and difficulty builds up incrementally to a mastery of the assessment objectives outlined at the start. Children's progress can be summatively assessed using the assessment copymasters at the end of the section.

The sessions

Units are composed of a number of teaching 'sessions'. These teaching suggestions are very specific and detailed, and use the full range of teaching strategies required during the literacy hour: teacher-directed whole class, individual, pair and group work. Approximate times are suggested to enable you to fit the sessions into your literacy hour programme. In practice, of course, the times actually required will vary according to the children's ability and the way the sessions are going. You will find a key to the symbols used in the sessions on page v.

Within a unit, the sessions tend to increase in complexity. Particular sessions may be used independently of the overall unit for a particular purpose but the sessions within a unit are closely linked, being designed to provide a complete teaching programme that combines reading and writing fiction and poetry with best practice in teaching literacy skills. You will probably want to teach the sessions within the context of their whole units.

The copymasters

Photocopiable sheets can be found at the end of every unit and these are integral to teaching the sessions. As well as providing activities and information, they also include extract and assessment sheets. Although a book of this kind cannot provide all the reading materials required to deliver the strategy, it should not be necessary to seek out many extra resources to deliver the targeted literacy objectives. All the copymasters are reinforced by structured lesson plans.

Using this book alongside the National Literacy Strategy and the Scottish Guidelines

You will find a National Literacy Strategy planner for each term's work after the section introduction. This details the term's work and shows where you can find units and sessions to resource it. You will find that the learning targets closely follow the content and wording of the fiction and poetry requirements for Years 5 and 6 in the National Literacy Strategy document.

Each unit of work can supply the material for a string of literacy hours. Units can be broken up into their constituent sessions across the week, using the timings as an approximate guide. Many of the activities and sessions can be used very flexibly and differentiation within the sessions is as much by outcome as by activity. Every teacher will, of course, interpret the demands of the literacy hour individually in the light of their own situation.

Despite its Literacy Strategy structure, all the ideas in the book are equally applicable to the Scottish situation: they are, in essence, structured and effective ideas for good practice in literacy teaching in all situations. You will find an outline planner linking the book to the Scottish English Language 5–14 Guidelines on the next page.

For teachers in Scotland, we have mapped the overall contents of the book against the attainment targets at Levels C–E, for reading, writing and talking. Necessarily a very wide range of attainment can often be covered by any one session, unit or section. The correlations below are for general guidance only. Because this book focuses on fiction and poetry, awareness of a wide range of genres is not a key feature. The key writing focus is very much on imaginative writing.

READING

Reading for enjoyment

Level C: Read regularly for enjoyment and give an opinion on texts of different kinds: Sections 1-3.

Level D: Read regularly for enjoyment texts with a range of subject matter and, with some support, reflect on what has been read and record personal reactions: Sections 1-6.

Level E: Read regularly for enjoyment texts with a wide range of subject matter, and provide either orally or in writing a considered personal view of the texts read, supported by some relevant evidence: Sections 3-6.

Reading to reflect on the writer's ideas and craft

Level C: Read a variety of straightforward texts, and in discussion and writing show that they understand the main and supporting ideas, and can draw conclusions from the text where appropriate: Sections 1-3.

Level D: Read a variety of texts, and in discussion and writing show that they understand the gist of the text, its main ideas and/or feelings, and can obtain particular information; and comment on the simpler aspects of the writer's craft: Sections 1-6.

Level E: Read independently, skim and scan to locate main points of a text; make predictions, identify subsidiary ideas; comment briefly on the opinions and attitudes of the writer; describe, with some direction, the simpler aspects of style and its intended audience: Sections 3-6.

Awareness of genre (type of text)

Level C: Identify a few obvious features of form and content in different types of text: stories, poems, dramatic texts, newspaper items, informational and reference texts: Section 1 Unit 3; Section 2 Unit 1, 2, 3.

Level D: Identify some similarities and differences of form and content in examples of the same type of text, for example ghost stories or letters of complaint or short biographical items from an encyclopaedia: Section 2 Unit 1, 2, 3; Section 5 Unit 1.

Level E: Identify some similarities and differences of form and content in examples of texts from a variety of genres, and comment on how these reflect the texts' purposes: Section 6 Unit 1, 2.

Knowledge about language

Level C: Show that they know, understand and can use at least the following terms: fiction, non-fiction, thesaurus, reference book; plot, dialogue, main character, conflict; verse, paragraph, headline; speech marks, exclamation mark: Sections 1-3.

Level D: Show that they know, understand and can use at least the following terms: theme, character, relationships, setting, motives; fact and opinion; layout, bold and italic type: Sections 1-6.

Level E: Show that they know, understand and can use at least the following terms: genre; syllable, root, stem, prefix, suffix; simile, metaphor: Sections 3-6.

WRITING

Imaginative writing

Level C: Write a brief, imaginative story, poem or play, using appropriate organisation and vocabulary: Section 1 Unit 2, 3; Section 2 Unit 1, 2, 3; Section 3 Unit 1, 3.

Level D: Write imaginative pieces in various genres, using appropriate organisation and vocabulary: Section 1 Unit 2, 3; Section 2 Unit 1, 2, 3; Section 3 Unit 1, 2, 3; Section 4 Unit 1, 2.

Level E: Write imaginative pieces in various genres, making some use of appropriate literary conventions: Section 4 Unit 1, 2; Section 5 Unit 2; Section 6 Unit 1, 2.

TALKING

Talking about texts

Level C: Talk about a range of stories, poems and dramatic texts that have been read, offering a personal response to the feelings or attitudes of those involved in the text: Section 1 Unit 1, 2; Section 2 Unit 2, 3.

Level D: Talk about a wide range of stories, poems and dramatic texts that have been heard or read, offering a personal response to some of the more complex feelings or attitudes of those involved in the text: Section 2 Unit 2, 3; Section 3 Unit 1; Section 4 Unit 1; Section 5 Unit 1, 2.

Level E: Talk readily about a wide range of stories, poems and dramatic texts, showing some appreciation of the differing viewpoints of the characters, or some awareness of what the author thinks about them: Section 3 Unit 1; Section 4 Unit 1; Section 5 Unit 1, 2; Section 6 Unit 1.

YEAR 5 TERM 1

Focus

In this section the children will be given the opportunity to:

1 Evaluate novels and stories and record their opinions
2 Investigate how characters are presented and use reading models to enhance the portrayal of characters in their own stories
3 Analyse and create playscripts.

Content

Unit 1: Evaluating novels and stories
Unit 2: Portraying characters
Unit 3: Playscripts

Extract list

Bawden, Nina: *The Angel of the Central Line*
Byars, Betsy: *The Summer of Swans*
Dickens, Charles: *A Christmas Carol*
King, Clive: *Stig of the Dump*
Storr, Catherine: *Clever Polly and the Stupid Wolf*
Wilde, Oscar: *Lady Windermere's Fan*

Assessment

Assessment Copymasters 12 and 13 are at the end of the section.

Copymaster 12 The Summer of Swans (1)

Copymaster 13 The Summer of Swans (2)

Curriculum Planner
National Literacy Strategy Planner

This chart shows you how to find activities by unit to resource your term's requirements for text level work on fiction. The Learning Targets closely follow the structure of the fiction requirements for the term in the National Literacy Strategy document (pages 44–45). A few of the requirements are not covered.

YEAR 5 Term 1

Range

Fiction:

* novels, stories and poems by significant children's writers
* playscripts.

TEXT LEVEL WORK

COMPREHENSION AND COMPOSITION

Reading comprehension

Pupils should be taught:

3 to investigate how characters are presented, referring to the text:
  * through dialogue, action and description;
  * how the reader responds to them (as victims, heroes, etc.);
  * through examining their relationships with other characters; Unit 2

5 to understand dramatic conventions including:
  * the conventions of scripting (e.g. stage directions, asides);
  * how character can be communicated in words and gesture;
  * how tension can be built up through pace, silences and delivery; Unit 3

9 to develop an active attitude towards reading: seeking answers, anticipating events, empathising with characters and imagining events that are described; Unit 1

10 to evaluate a book by referring to details and examples in the text; Unit 1

Writing composition

Pupils should be taught:

13 to record their ideas, reflections and predictions about a book, e.g. through a reading log or journal; Unit 1

15 to write new scenes or characters into a story, in the manner of the writer, maintaining consistency of character and style, using paragraphs to organise and develop detail; Unit 2

18 to write own playscript, applying conventions learned from reading, include production notes; Unit 3

19 to annotate a section of playscript as a preparation for performance, taking into account pace, movement, gesture and delivery of lines and the needs of the audience; Unit 3

UNIT 1 | Evaluating novels and stories

Learning targets

On completion of this unit the children should be able to:

1 ➤➤ develop an active attitude towards reading: seeking answers, anticipating events, empathising with characters and imagining events that are described

2 ➤➤ evaluate a book by referring to details and examples in the text

3 ➤➤ record their ideas, reflections and predictions about a book, e.g. through a reading log or journal.

Before you start

Background knowledge

These objectives are quite ambitious in as much as the children's response to stories and novels is probably still at the stage of 'I liked/didn't like it'! The aim of this unit is to provide a structure to support the children's reading. The sessions help the children to engage with the texts in formulating predictions and evaluative responses.

Resources for Session 1

Copymaster 1 Book reports

Resources for Session 2

Copymaster 2 Our predictions
Copymaster 3 What might happen next?

Links to other units

Learning Targets: Fiction and Poetry Years 3 and 4
Year 3 Term 3 Unit 1: Story openings

Assessment indicators

- Can the children articulate their responses to novels and stories giving reasons for their opinions?
- Can they record their thoughts and feelings about a novel or story in writing?
- Can they discuss a storyline in terms of what has happened and what then might happen as a result?

Teaching the sessions

Session 1 ② ③

Introduction 20-30min

▦ Begin by discussing what the children do if they have just finished a good book, e.g.

- Look for another book by the same author?
- Tell a friend how good it was?
- Retell the story to someone?

Ask for examples of books the children have enjoyed and discuss why they enjoyed them, e.g.

- evoked a particular response
- identified with a particular character
- kept the reader guessing until the very end.

Ask for examples of books the children have not enjoyed and investigate why. The most likely answer

at this point is 'it was boring' so probe more deeply to encourage the children to articulate the reasons as to what *exactly* they didn't like.

If you have been using a particular novel or story as a class reader, discuss the children's thoughts and feelings about it, asking the children to give reasons for their opinions.

Discuss with the children the merits of keeping a reading diary:

- What should it include?
    - title
    - author
    - publisher
    - characters
    - brief synopsis of the plot
    - thoughts and feelings about the book
- Why might it be useful?
    - it makes the reader think back (reflect) on

what he/she has read and reach a conclusion as to why the book was enjoyable or not
- Who would find it useful?
  the writer - as a personal record
  other people - as a source of information about books they might like to read.

Book reports 20-30min

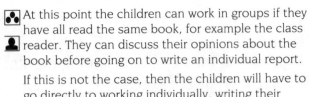 At this point the children can work in groups if they have all read the same book, for example the class reader. They can discuss their opinions about the book before going on to write an individual report.

If this is not the case, then the children will have to go directly to working individually, writing their reflections on a novel or story they have recently finished.

Give each child **Copymaster 1 Book reports**. Go through the sections ensuring that the children understand what is required.

- Title and author: found on the front cover of the book
- Publisher: found on the first page or on the back cover
- Important characters: the children must use their judgement to select only the main characters and not write an entire cast list!
  A few details about each main character should be included, e.g. Scrooge – an old, bad-tempered businessman
- Brief outline of the plot: children have a tendency to record 'chapter and verse'. Explain that an outline is a brief summary of the events in the story, not a detailed account of everything that happens. Point out the limited space there is for this part of the report. It is a good idea to make notes and write these up into a short outline.
- The part of the story I liked best … because: the important part here is the 'because'. Stress that just writing 'it was frightening/exciting/funny', etc. is not enough. The children must ask themselves *why* the episode was 'frightening/exciting/funny', etc. and give reasons.
- I liked the book because: again, stress that you want to know *why*.
- I did not like the book because: this is a good opportunity to point out that they are perfectly entitled to dislike a book. Just because something is published does not mean that it is good! They must, however, give detailed reasons why they disliked it, e.g. 'it was predictable/unbelievable', 'the characters did not come across as 'real' so I didn't care what happened to them', etc.

The completed book reports can be kept in a file as a class reference.

Filling in book report sheets can be an ongoing activity but do not make it an automatic task after *every* book read. Encourage the children to record their thoughts and feelings in this form if they have particularly enjoyed or disliked a book. Whenever possible, precede this activity with some discussion of the book as a class, group or individually, whichever is appropriate.

Session 2

Introduction 20min

 Explain to the children that reading becomes a more exciting activity if they get involved in the story by trying to anticipate what might happen next. This is a good opportunity to discuss why novels are written in chapters and why each chapter ends where it does. This is usually at a crucial point in the story and the reader wants to read on to find out what happens.

Use the class reader to discuss:
- what has happened so far
- what *might* happen next.

In theory, of course, *anything* might happen but the children should be prompted to make a link between past events and *likely* future events.

Make a list of the children's predictions and then read on to find out what does happen.

Our predictions 20-30min

 Give each group **Copymaster 2 Our predictions**. This is the beginning of a short story by Nina Bawden called T*he Angel of the Central Line*. The children should read the extract carefully and discuss what they think might happen next.

Summary 10min

 Discuss the children's predictions, investigating why they thought of a particular series of events. What clues in the extract lead them to come to these conclusions?

If time allows, read the rest of the story to the children. It is published in *Just in Time – Stories to Mark the Millennium* by Puffin Books.

What might happen next? 20min

 Copymaster 3 What might happen next? can be used by the children for their individual reading and gives them a structure for predicting the next event(s) in their book.

Title: _____

Author:_____

Publisher: _____

Important characters:_____

_____

_____

Brief outline of the plot: _____

_____

_____

_____

The part of the story I liked best was: _____

_____

_____

_____

This was because: _____

_____

_____

_____

I liked the book because: _____

_____

_____

_____

I did not like the book because: _____

_____

_____

_____

The Angel of the Central Line

This is a true story. I tell you this because I am afraid that otherwise you won't believe it. (I find it quite hard to believe myself, which is why I am writing it down so that later on in my life, when I am old, I will be able to read it and remind myself that it really happened.)

I had quarrelled with my best friend, Tom. It was the middle of winter. He lived in Notting Hill and I lived in Islington, but at that time, which was before the collapse of the cities, most outlying settlements were connected by the London Underground Railway, or, as we called it then, the tube.

I won't say what we quarrelled about because it has nothing to do with my story. All you need to know is that we had been sitting in a café close by Notting Hill Gate tube station when he said he never wanted to see me again in this life, and I said that I hoped I would never have to see him again in the next.

All the way home in the tube train I wished I was dead. As I opened the front door I heard the phone ringing and ran to answer it, but it stopped as I got there. 'Just as well,' my dad said, coming out of the kitchen. 'I told your mother we'd go to Tesco before she got back and we're running behind.' …

There were three messages on the answer phone.

The first said, 'Just thought I'd ring.'

The second, 'You ought to be home by now. Oh, *all right*! I'm *sorry*. OK?'

The third message was longer. 'Look. Listen. I'm going to the café now. It's twenty to six. I'll wait there till seven. If you don't come, OK, I'll just know that's *it*. Right?' And the phone was slammed down.

Our predictions (cont.)

It was just before six o'clock now. It wouldn't take more than forty minutes once I got to the station; there were plenty of trains at rush hour. I yelled at Dad in the kitchen and he yelled back. I was not to be later than nine o'clock, it was a school day tomorrow, I knew the rules! And wrap up – the barometer was dropping like a stone.

He was right about that. It was freezing outside, ice underfoot and vicious needles of sleet slashing horizontally into my face. I kept my head down, slipping and slithering, but I managed to stay upright. Then I was in the warmth of the Underground station and crashing down the escalators to the Northern Line.

There was a train waiting. I got in, but only just: lucky I'm thin, I thought. Even so, there wasn't much room to breath … There were only two stops between the Angel station and Bank, which was where I had to change for the Central Line to Notting Hill Gate. Bank was a huge underground station, miles of dim, leaking tunnels and crumbling spiral stairs … I knew Bank station. I could have found my way blindfold; up and down, in and out, from the Northern to the Central Line and back again. But this evening the tunnels and stairs were more crowded – and much smellier – than usual. When I started to climb the last flight of dark, winding stairs, there were so many people thundering down them that I had to cling on to the rail at the side with both hands to avoid being knocked over and trampled to death underfoot.

I heard the voice over the Tannoy: '… a serious fire at Stratford. There will be no more trains on the Central Line tonight.'

From *The Angel of the Central Line* by Nina Bawden

3 | What might happen next?

The story so far ... _____

_____

_____

_____

_____

What I think might happen ... _____

_____

_____

_____

_____

What could also happen ... _____

_____

_____

_____

Read on ...
Were you correct? What *did* happen? _____

_____

_____

Portraying characters

Learning targets

On completion of this unit the children should be able to:

1 ➤➤ investigate how characters are presented, referring to the text:
   - through dialogue, action and description
   - how the reader responds to them (as victims, heroes, etc.)
   - through examining their relationships with other characters

2 ➤➤ write new scenes or characters into a story, in the manner of the writer, maintaining consistency of character and style, using paragraphs to organise and develop detail.

Before you start

Background knowledge

In *Learning Targets: Fiction and Poetry Years 3 and 4*, the children have investigated character in the context of historical and traditional stories. Increasingly, the objectives are based on children reading complete stories and novels, in this case, by significant children's writers. These sessions, based on extracts, give the opportunity to concentrate on character portrayal and will equip the children with a method of examining character which they can use in their extended reading.

Resources for Session 1

Copymaster 4 A Christmas Carol

Resources for Session 2

Copymaster 5 Clever Polly and the Stupid Wolf

Copymaster 6 Stig of the Dump
Copymaster 7 Analysing character

Links to other units

Learning Targets: Fiction and Poetry Years 3 and 4
Year 3 Term 2 Unit 2: Characters
Year 4 Term 1 Unit 1: Characters

Assessment indicators

- Can the children analyse characters in stories in terms of dialogue and action?
- Can they articulate their response to characters?
- Can they include characters in their stories which are presented to the reader in ways other than direct author description?
- Can they write character descriptions to evoke a given response?

Teaching the sessions

Session 1 ① ②

Introduction   10–15 min

▨ Begin by discussing 'characters' in the context of stories with the children.
- What do they understand by the term 'character'?
- In what ways can an author present characters to the reader?

The children will probably respond by saying that the author can tell the reader what a character looks like and what sort of person he/she is. They may need prompting to consider:

- what a character says
- what a character does
- how other characters respond to him/her

as ways in which a reader can get to know a character in a story.

Analysing characters

20-25 min

Give each child **Copymaster 4 A Christmas Carol**. Some of the children may be familiar with the story but all they need to know at this point is that the novel was written and is set in Victorian times. The extract takes place just before Christmas when Scrooge's nephew is visiting his uncle at work. There is space available at the bottom of the copymaster for the children to make notes about the characters.

In groups, the children should:

- read through the extract
- discuss the two characters, looking for clues in the extract as to what sort of person each one is and how the reader knows this.

Scrooge's nephew – what we learn through:

- his conversation: he says things in a 'cheerful voice' and 'gaily'; he looks on the bright side of life; he does not view everything in terms of money
- his reaction to his uncle: he doesn't get angry or sullen even though Scrooge is rude; he tries to cheer up Scrooge
- other characters: Scrooge says of him 'You're poor enough'.

Scrooge – what we learn through:

- his conversation: the whole of Scrooge's conversation shows him to be bad-tempered and thoroughly unpleasant; he sees everything in terms of money
- his reaction to his nephew: he doesn't seem to be pleased to see him; Scrooge reminds him he is poor and has no right to be merry
- other characters: Scrooge's nephew says 'You're rich enough'.

Summary

10 min

Discuss the groups' findings through class discussion. What have they concluded about each character? In what ways have they found out information about each character?

Gathering these clues about the characters will help the children to understand the importance of reader response. Discuss with the children how they feel about:

- Scrooge
- Scrooge's nephew.

The children should understand that an author portrays a character in a certain way in order to get the reader to like, dislike, admire, feel sorry for, feel frightened of, etc. that character.

Written assignments

30+ min

The children can be given a variety of written character assignments based on the extract from *A Christmas Carol*. Encourage them to work in draft form initially and discuss the work in progress.

1 In your own words, write character descriptions of Scrooge and his nephew, including detail of how the author makes you feel about each character.

2 Continue the conversation between Scrooge and his nephew. This could include why Scrooge's nephew has visited his uncle and how Scrooge reacts when he discovers the reason why.

3 Introduce a new character into the scene. Decide what sort of person this new character is and inform the reader through what he/she says and does and how Scrooge and his nephew respond to him/her. Make sure you know how you want your reader to respond to this new character.

Homework

The children can complete their written assignment for homework.

Session 2

Copymaster 5 and **Copymaster 6** give further extracts from significant children's writers on which character analysis can be based. They can be used for whole class sessions or group work.

Copymaster 7 gives the children a frame for writing notes on characters.

A Christmas Carol

'A merry Christmas, uncle! God save you!' cried a cheerful voice. It was the voice of Scrooge's nephew, who came upon him so quickly that this was the first intimation he had of his approach.

'Bah!' said Scrooge, 'Humbug!'

He had so heated himself with rapid walking in the fog and frost, this nephew of Scrooge's, that he was all in a glow; his face was ruddy and handsome; his eyes sparkled, and his breath smoked again.

'Christmas a humbug, uncle!' said Scrooge's nephew, 'You don't mean that, I am sure?'

'I do,' said Scrooge. 'Merry Christmas! What right have you to be merry? What reason have you to be merry? You're poor enough.'

'Come, then,' returned the nephew gaily. 'What right have you to be dismal? What reason have you to be morose? You're rich enough.'

Scrooge having no better answer ready on the spur of the moment, said, 'Bah!' again; and followed it up with 'Humbug.'

'Don't be cross, uncle!' said the nephew.

'What else can I be,' returned the uncle, 'when I live in such a world of fools as this? Merry Christmas! Out upon merry Christmas! What's Christmas time to you but a time for paying bills without money; a time for finding yourself a year older, but not an hour richer; a time for balancing your books and having every item in 'em through a round dozen of months presented dead against you? If I could work my will,' said Scrooge indignantly, 'every idiot who goes around with 'Merry Christmas' on his lips should be boiled with his own pudding, and buried with a stake of holly through his heart. He should!'

'Uncle!' pleaded the nephew.

'Nephew!' returned the uncle, sternly, 'keep Christmas in your own way, and let me keep it in mine.'

'Keep it!' repeated Scrooge's nephew. 'But you don't keep it.'

'Let me leave it alone, then,' said Scrooge. 'Much good may it do you! Much good it has ever done you!'

A Christmas Carol (cont.)

'There are many things from which I might have derived good, by which I have not profited, I dare say,' returned the nephew. 'Christmas among the rest. But I am sure I have always thought of Christmas time, when it has come round … as a good time; a kind, forgiving, charitable, pleasant time … And therefore, uncle, though it has never put a scrap of gold or silver in my pocket, I believe that it *has* done me good, and *will* do me good; and I say, God bless it!'

From *A Christmas Carol* by Charles Dickens

Notes about the characters:

Clever Polly and the Stupid Wolf

This is a series of stories in which Polly is visited several times by a wolf. In this extract from 'Huff Puff' make notes on what you find out about the characters of Polly and the wolf.

It was a very calm and sunny day when Polly heard a most peculiar noise outside the house. It sounded like a small storm. She could hear the wind whistling round the corner of the house, but when she looked up at the treetops they were not even swaying; everything was perfectly still …

Polly went to the sitting-room window which looked out in front of the house, but she could see nothing. She went to the kitchen at the back of the house and looked out.

She saw the wolf. He was leaning against the garden wall and fanning himself with a large leaf off a plane tree. He looked hot and exhausted. As Polly looked, he stopped fanning, threw away the leaf, and began some extraordinary contortions.

First he bent himself double and straightened up again. Then he made one or two huge bites at nothing and appeared to swallow some large mouthfuls of air. Then he threw back his head and snorted loudly. Finally he bent double again and started to breathe in. As he breathed in he stood up and swelled out. He swelled and he swelled till from being a thin black wolf he became quite a fat black wolf, and his chest was as round as a barrel.

Then he blew.

'So that was the extraordinary noise,' Polly said to herself. She opened the kitchen window and leant out. The curtains blew about behind her in the wolf-made wind.

'What are you doing, Wolf?' she called out to him, as his breath gave out and the noise got less.

'Practising,' the wolf said airily. 'Just practising.'

'What for?'

'Blowing your house down, of course.'

'Blowing down this house?' Polly asked. 'This house? But you couldn't. It's much too solid.'

'It looks solid I admit,' the wolf said. 'But I know that's all sham. And if I go on practising

I'll get plenty of push in my blow and then one day – Heigh Presto! (that's what they always said in books,' he added) – 'over it will topple and I shall eat you up.'

'But this is a brick house,' Polly objected.

'Well, I know it looks like brick, but it can't really be brick. It's mud really, isn't it now?'

'You're thinking of the three little pigs,' said Polly. 'They built their houses of mud and sticks, the first two did, didn't they?'

'Well, yes I am,' the wolf admitted. 'But there's only one of you so I thought you'd probably build three houses. One of mud, and the next of sticks, and then a brick one.'

'This is the brick one,' said Polly firmly.

'Did you build the others first?' asked the wolf.

'No, I didn't. And I didn't build this one either. I just came to live in it.'

'You're sure it's not mud underneath that sort of brick pattern?' asked the wolf anxiously. 'Because when I was huffing and puffing just now, it seemed to me to give a sort of wobble. As if it might fall down some time if I blew hard enough.'

Polly felt a little frightened, but she was fairly sure the wolf couldn't blow down a brick house, so she said, 'Try again and let me see.'

The wolf doubled himself up, filled himself out and then blew with all his might. The blades of grass and the rose bushes and the clean washing waved madly in the wind, but the house never stirred at all.

'No,' said Polly, very much relieved. 'You aren't blowing down this house. It really is brick and I don't see why you should expect to be able to blow down a brick house.'

From *Clever Polly and the Stupid Wolf* by Catherine Storr

Stig of the Dump

Barney meets Stig – a caveboy who lives in a chalk pit – and they have many adventures together. In this extract Barney and Stig have chased some thieves and Barney is returning his Grandmother's silver along with lots of other stolen property. Read the extract and make notes on the characters of Barney, his Granny and the policeman.

Granny and Lou were back from shopping when Barney struggled in through the front gate carrying the two heavy suitcases full of silver.

'Barney, what on earth have you been up to?' Granny exclaimed.

'I've brought your spoons and forks back, Granny. You see two men came to do the television. I mean that's what they said, but they were thieves really and I was up the tree but me and Stig chased them away and I let their car go over into the chalk pit, and it's there now with all the treasure in it.'

'Well, you have been having fun,' said Granny. 'Now let's have tea, shall we. Lay the table Lou, and Barney, go and wash your hands. Look at them!' …

When Barney got back there was a policeman at the door talking to Granny. She looked worried.

'What's this about thieves, sonny?' asked the policeman.

'Yes, I saw them up the tree, I mean *I* was, and one of them went into the house, and I went to fetch my friend Stig, and me and Stig had a fight with them and they ran away and the teaspoons fell out and the car was full of treasure.'

The policeman scratched his head. 'Ah now, a *car*, you say. Just where might this car be?'

Barney stood on one leg. 'Well, I thought perhaps I could drive it to the police station, but it went backwards over the cliff and Stig thought it was dead and started skinning it and then we buried it. But I couldn't *help* it, I *promise!*'

The policeman was trying to write all this down in a notebook, but when he got to the part about skinning and burying the car he stopped writing and looked hard at Barney.

'You wouldn't be making this up, would you son?' he asked sternly.

'I'm afraid my grandson has a very strong imagination,' said Granny.

'But I'm telling the truth, Granny! I *promise!*' said Barney.

'Perhaps the little boy would like to show me where this, er, alleged treasure is, ma'am,' suggested the policeman.

'Yes, yes' cried Barney. 'It's just down the lane. Come on!' And he took the policeman by the hand and pulled him through the front gate, and down the lane, explaining as he went.

'It's all in the bottom of the car, the treasure. Or, well, it's in the top of the car I suppose because the car's upside down in the bottom of the pit.'

He led the way to the top of the cliff where the car had gone over and pointed. 'It's down there,' he said.

The policeman looked over. 'I can't see nothing,' he said.

'Of course not,' explained Barney. 'We buried it. Come on down and see.'

The policeman looked more and more disbelieving. 'Look, son,' he said. 'There's three houses been burgled in the district, and it's my job to catch the thieves and get the valuables back. And I haven't got a lot of time to waste. What about this treasure of yours?'

'It's *down* there,' Barney insisted. 'I'll show it to you if you just come down.'

From *Stig of the Dump* by Clive King

An example of what the character says ...

_____

_____

_____

_____

This tells me ...

_____

_____

_____

_____

An example of what the character does ...

_____

_____

_____

_____

This tells me ...

_____

_____

_____

_____

Example of what another character says about him/her ...

_____

_____

_____

_____

This tells me ...

_____

_____

_____

_____

How I feel about this character ... _____

_____

_____

Playscripts

Learning targets

On completion of this unit the children should be able to:

1 ➤➤ understand dramatic conventions including:
- the conventions of scripting (e.g. stage directions, asides)
- how character can be communicated in words and gesture
- how tension can be built up through pace, silences and delivery

2 ➤➤ write own playscript, applying conventions learned from reading; include production notes

3 ➤➤ annotate a section of playscript as a preparation for performance, taking into account pace, movement, gesture and delivery of lines and the needs of the audience.

Before you start

Background knowledge

If the children have not worked through the activities in Year 4 Term 1 Unit 2 (see Links to other units), then they should do so before tackling the work in this unit.

The children should be familiar with dramatic conventions such as dialogue, setting and simple stage directions. This unit is based on a very short extract from Oscar Wilde's *Lady Windermere's Fan* which provides an annotated script on which the children can model their own work.

Resources for Session 1

Copymaster 8   The persons of the play
Copymaster 9   Lady Windermere's Fan
Copymaster 10 Annotating a playscript

Resources for Session 2

Copymaster 11 Planning notes for plays

Links to other units

Learning Targets: Reading and Writing Key Stage 1
Section 3: Plays
Learning Targets: Fiction and Poetry Years 3 and 4
Year 4 Term 1 Unit 2: Playscripts

Assessment indicators

- Can the children respond to dramatic conventions when reading a play?
- Can they model their own playscripts on those read in terms of page layout and dramatic conventions?

Teaching the sessions

Session 1 ① ③

Introduction
20-30min

Recap on the work the children have done in earlier units on playscripts.
- How does a playscript look different from a story on the page?
- What is the difference between reading a story and seeing it acted on the stage or television?
- What do the children understand by the terms dialogue, stage direction, setting, props, character and plot?

Explain that you are going to look at the opening pages of a play written by Oscar Wilde in 1893 called *Lady Windermere's Fan*. Give each child **Copymaster 8 The persons of the play**, and discuss it with them.

- What information does this first page give?
- What are 'the persons of the play'?
- Why do they think it is important for the playwright to give this information to the people who are going to put on the play?

Give the children **Copymaster 9 Lady Windermere's Fan**, and read through it with them.

Discuss the various information contained on the page in terms of layout, use of italics, use of brackets, etc.:

- the setting
- the characters
- the dialogue
- the stage directions.

What do the children understand by:

- 'Doors C and R' (centre and right of stage)
- 'small tea-table L' (left of stage)
- 'Exit C' (go out through door centre stage).

Explain to the children that 'L' and 'R' refers to the actor's left or right as he/she stands on the stage facing the audience.

From reading the script, ask the children to help you compile a props list: roses, blue bowl and fan.

Acting the scene

 Put the children into groups of three and ask them to rehearse the short extract. It is not necessary that they learn the lines but they should take careful notice of the stage directions for:

- their actions
- the way they say their lines
- exits and entrances on to the stage.

While the children are rehearsing, draw their attention to clues in the dialogue which will help them interpret what the characters are doing.

- 'No, I can't shake hands with you' indicates Lord Darlington has offered his hand to Lady Windermere.
- 'And what a wonderful fan!' indicates that Lord Darlington is looking around the room.

Summary `30 min`

 If possible, use a hall or any large space for the children to act out the scene.

Annotating a playscript `20-25 min`

 Copymaster 10 Annotating a playscript gives the children the opportunity to add details of the setting and stage directions to a simple script. Explain to the children that they are not trying to 'guess' the right answers. The set and the interpretation of the

way the characters move and speak is entirely up to them. The aim of the activity is to give as much helpful information as possible. Encourage them to make a sketch of how they want the stage to look before they begin their annotations so they can include the conventions of R/C/L for entrances and exits.

Session 2

Introduction `10 min`

 Recap on what the children have learned about dramatic conventions and explain to them that they are going to work in groups to write the first scene of a play.

You may wish to give them a story line, number of characters, etc., or you may wish to let each group decide for itself.

Writing a scene `30 min`

 In groups the children should discuss:

- what their scene is to be about – the action
- where it takes place – the set
- the list of characters – people in the play.

Copymaster 11 Planning notes for plays will support the children in this activity.

When these things have been decided upon they can then write the lines of dialogue along with the necessary stage directions. Encourage them to work in draft form as there will be changes as the script progresses.

Characters `20 min`

 This activity can be set for homework. Each child should make an annotated drawing of their character. The annotations will explain the costume needed for the part, and words and phrases to describe:

- who the character is
- the personality of the character
- his/her part in the play.

Some time should be set aside for the children to act their scenes.

THE PERSONS OF THE PLAY:

Lord Windermere

Lord Darlington

Lord Augustus Lorton

Mr Dumby

Mr Cecil Graham

Mr Hopper

Parker, Butler

Lady Windermere

The Duchess of Berwick

Lady Agatha Carlisle

Lady Plymdale

Lady Stutfield

Lady Jedburgh

Mrs Cowper-Cowper

Mrs Erlynne

Rosalie, Maid

THE SCENES OF THE PLAY:

ACT I.	Morning-room in Lord Windermere's house.
ACT II.	Drawing-room in Lord Windermere's house.
ACT III.	Lord Darlington's rooms.
ACT IV.	Same as Act 1.

TIME: *The Present*.

PLACE: *London*.

The action of the play takes place within twenty-four hours, beginning on a Tuesday afternoon at five o'clock, and ending the next day at 1.30 p.m.

Lady Windermere's Fan

FIRST ACT

SCENE

Morning-room of Lord Windermere's house in Carlton House Terrace. Doors C and R. Bureau with books and papers R. Sofa with small tea-table L. Window opening on to terrace L. Table R.

Lady Windermere is at table R, arranging roses in a blue bowl.

Enter Parker

Parker: Is your ladyship at home this afternoon?

Lady Windermere: Yes – who has called?

Parker: Lord Darlington, my lady.

Lady Windermere: [*Hesitates for a moment.*] Show him up – and I'm at home to any one who calls.

Parker: Yes, my lady. [*Exit C.*]

Lady Windermere: It's best for me to see him before to-night. I'm glad he's come.

Enter Parker C.

Parker: Lord Darlington.

Enter Lord Darlington C. [*Exit Parker.*]

Lord Darlington: How do you do, Lady Windermere?

Lady Windermere: How do you do, Lord Darlington? No, I can't shake hands with you. My hands are all wet with these roses. Aren't they lovely? They came up from Selby this morning.

Lord Darlington: They are quite perfect. [*Sees a fan lying on the table.*] And what a wonderful fan! May I look at it?

Lady Windermere: Do. Pretty, isn't it! It's got my name on it, and everything. I have only just seen it myself. It's my husband's birthday present to me. You know to-day is my birthday?

Lord Darlington: No? Is it really?

Lady Windermere: Yes, I'm of age to-day. Quite an important day in my life, isn't it? That is why I am giving this party to-night. Do sit down. [*Still arranging flowers.*]

Lord Darlington: [*Sitting down.*] I wish I had known it was your birthday, Lady Windermere. I would have covered the whole street in front of your house with flowers for you to walk on. They are made for you.

SCENE

_____

_____

_____

Mr Clark is _____

John: [_____.] Can I help you?

Mr Clark: Ah, yes. I came in last week. You ordered a book for me.

John: Your name, sir?

Mr Clark: [_____.] You should know my name, I've
                   been coming here for years!

John: [_____.] I've only been working here for a
                   few weeks, sir.

Mr Clark: [_____.] The name's Clark.

John: And the title of the book sir?

Mr Clark: 'The Worst Journey in the World'.

John: Do have a seat sir and I will go and look.

                   John _____.
                   Mr Clarke _____.

Continue the dialogue and action when John returns without the book.

11 | Planning notes for plays

What is the scene about? _____

_____

_____

_____

What will the stage look like?

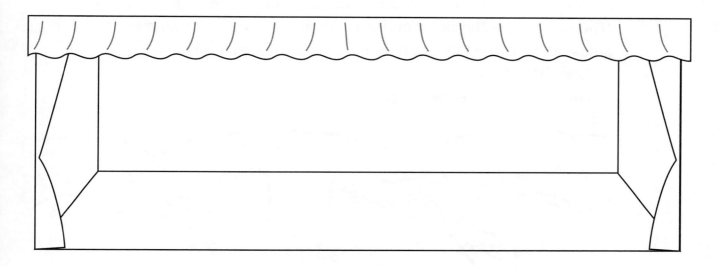

Who are the characters? _____

_____

_____

_____

What props will you need? _____

_____

_____

_____

Sara Godfrey was lying on the bed tying a scarf on the dog, Boysie. 'Hold your chin up, Boysie, will you?' she said as she braced herself on one elbow. The dog was old, slept all the time, and he was lying on his side with his eyes closed while she lifted his head and tied the scarf.

Her sister Wanda was sitting at the dressing-table combing her hair. Wanda said, 'Why don't you leave Boysie alone?'

'There's nothing else to do,' Sara answered without looking up. 'You want to see a show?'

'Not particularly.'

'It's called "The Many Faces of Boysie."'

'Now I know I don't want to see it.'

Sara held up the dog with the scarf neatly tied beneath his chin and said, 'The first face of Boysie, proudly presented for your entertainment and amusement, is the Russian Peasant Woman. Taaaaaa-daaaaaa!'

'Leave the dog alone.'

'He likes to be in shows, don't you, Boysie?'

She untied the scarf, refolded it and set it carefully on top of the dog's head. 'And now for the second face of Boysie, we travel half-way around the world to the mysterious East, where we see Boysie the Inscrutable Hindu. Taaaaaa-daaaaaa!'

With a sigh Wanda turned and looked at the dog. 'That's pathetic. In people's age that dog is eighty-four years old.' She shook a can of hair spray and sprayed her hair. 'And besides, that's my good scarf.'

'Oh, all right.' Sara fell back heavily against the pillow. 'I can't do anything around here.'

'Well, if it's going to make you that miserable, I'll watch the show.'

'I don't want to do it any more. It's no fun now. This place smells like a perfume factory.' She put the scarf over her face and stared up through the thin blue material. Beside her, Boysie lay back down and curled himself into a ball. They lay without moving for a moment and then Sara sat up on the bed and looked down at her long, lanky legs. She said, 'I have the biggest feet in my school.'

'Honestly, Sara, I hope you are not going to start listing all the millions of things wrong with you because I just don't want to hear it again.'

'Well, it's the truth about my feet. One time in Phys Ed the boys started throwing the girls' tennis shoes around and Bull Durham got my tennis shoes and put them on and they fit perfectly! How do you think it feels to wear the same size shoe as Bull Durham?'

'People don't notice things like that.'

'Huh!'

'No, they don't. I have perfectly terrible hands – look at my fingers – only I don't go around all the time saying, "Everybody, look at my stubby fingers, I have stubby fingers, everybody," to *make* people notice. You should just ignore things that are wrong with you. The truth is everyone else is so worried about what's wrong with *them* that –'

'It is very difficult to ignore the fact that you have huge feet when Bull Durham is dancing all over the gym in your shoes. They were not stretched the tiniest little bit when he took them off either.'

'You wear the same size shoe as Jackie Kennedy Onassis if that makes you feel any better.'

'How do you know?'

'Because one time when she was going into an Indian temple she had to leave her shoes outside and some reporter looked in them to see what size they were.' She leaned close to the mirror and looked at her teeth.

'Her feet *look* littler.'

'That's because she doesn't wear orange tennis shoes.'

'I like my orange tennis shoes.' Sara sat on the edge of the bed, slipped her feet into the shoes, and held them up. 'What's wrong with them?'

From *The Summer of Swans* by Betsy Byars

Read the opening extract from *The Summer of Swans*.

Predictions

- Summarise the story so far.
- Write what you think might happen next.

Your opinion

- Do you think you would like to read this book? Give your reasons.
- Do you think you would not like to read this book? Give your reasons.

Characters

We are introduced to the characters of Sara and Wanda at the beginning of the story.

- Write a paragraph about Sara explaining what sort of person you think she is and give reasons for your opinion.
- Write a paragraph about Wanda explaining what sort of person you think she is and give reasons for your opinion.

Playscript

Use the opening of this story as the basis for a playscript. Include:

- setting
- characters
- dialogue
- stage directions.

YEAR 5 TERM 2

Focus

In this section the children will be given the opportunity to:

1   Build on earlier work on myths, legends and traditional tales, concentrating on those stories by which ancient peoples sought to explain natural phenomenon.
2   Investigate various poetic forms, e.g. ballads and sonnets, and revise narrative poetry in the form of cautionary tales.
3   Look closely at one genre of popular fiction, e.g. science fiction.

Content

Unit 1: Traditional tales
Unit 2: Poetic forms
Unit 3: Science fiction

Extract list

Anastasio, Dina: *Apollo 13*
Belloc, Hilaire: 'Jim'
Clare, John: 'The Vixen'
Clark, Arthur C.: *Who's there?*
Coleridge, Samuel Taylor: *The Rime of the Ancient Mariner*
Guerber, H.A.: *The story of Prometheus*
Nye, Robert: *The origin of fire*
Shelley, Percy Bysshe: 'Ozymandias'
Squire, Sir John: 'There was an Indian'
Swindells, Robert: *Timesnatch*
Wells, H.G.: *The War of the Worlds*

Assessment

Assessment Copymasters 26–7 are at the end of the section.

Copymaster 26 *Timesnatch* (1)

Copymaster 27 *Timesnatch* (2)

This chart shows you how to find activities by unit to resource your term's requirements for text level work on fiction and poetry. The Learning Targets closely follow the structure of the fiction and poetry requirements for the term in the National Literacy Strategy document (pages 46–47). A few of the requirements are not covered.

YEAR 5 Term 2

Range

Fiction and poetry:
- traditional stories, myths, legends, fables from a range of cultures
- longer classic poetry, including narrative poetry.

TEXT LEVEL WORK

COMPREHENSION AND COMPOSITION

Reading comprehension

Pupils should be taught:

1 to identify and classify the features of myths, legends and fables; Unit 1

2 to investigate different versions of the same story in print or on film, identifying similarities and differences; recognise how stories change over time and differences of culture and place that are expressed in stories; Unit 1

4 to read a range of narrative poems; Unit 2

6 to understand terms which describe different kinds of poems, e.g. ballad, sonnet, rap, elegy, narrative poem, and to identify typical features; Unit 2

9 to investigate the features of different fiction genres, e.g. science fiction, adventure, discussing the appeal of popular fiction; Unit 3

Writing composition

Pupils should be taught:

11 to write own versions of legends, myths and fables, using structures and themes identified in reading; Unit 1

12 to use the structures of poems read to write extensions based on these, e.g. additional verses, or substituting own words and ideas; Unit 2

13 to review and edit writing to produce a final form, matched to the needs of an identified reader; Unit 3

Traditional tales

Learning targets

On completion of this unit the children should be able to:

1 ➤➤ identify and classify the features of myths, legends and fables
2 ➤➤ investigate different versions of the same story in print or on film, identifying similarities and differences; recognise how stories change over time and differences of culture and place that are expressed in stories
3 ➤➤ write own versions of legends, myths and fables, using structures and themes identified in reading.

Before you start

Background knowledge

The sessions in this unit build upon the work the children have done in Years 3 and 4 (see Links to other units) on traditional tales such as parables, legends, fables, etc.

A common theme that runs through traditional tales from many cultures is that of explaining how some phenomenon came to be, prior to the scientific explanations we have today. In this unit two legends of how man came to possess fire form the basis of investigating this theme. Other examples, such as the wide variety of creation stories, can be used to extend the children's knowledge of the early story telling traditions from many cultures. This will give the children stimulus material to compare and contrast, and provide models for their own writing.

Resources for Session 1

Copymaster 14 The story of Prometheus
Copymaster 15 The origin of fire

Resources for Session 2

Copymaster 16 Explaining

Links to other units

Learning Targets: Fiction and Poetry Years 3 and 4
Year 3 Term 2 Unit 1: Traditional stories
Year 3 Term 2 Unit 3: Story plans
Year 3 Term 3 Unit 1: Story openings

Assessment indicators

- Can the children recognise a traditional tale which explains a natural phenomenon?
- Can they plan and write a traditional tale which explains a natural phenomenon?

Teaching the sessions

Session 1 ① ②

Introduction   10-15 min

▨ Begin by recapping on what the children understand by the term 'traditional tale'. Discuss the various forms with which they are familiar:

- fairy story: a children's tale with a magical element
- a fable: a tale, especially with animal characters, conveying a moral
- a parable: a story to illustrate a moral or spiritual lesson
- a myth: traditional story usually containing supernatural beings, e.g. gods
- a legend: traditional story, thought to have some basis in truth.

Can the children give examples of each kind of traditional story?

Remind the children of the opening of the Greek legend of Phaethon (see page 29 of *Learning Targets: Fiction and Poetry Years 3 and 4*). It is a legend from Ancient Greece which seeks to explain the daily movement of the sun across the sky. Traditional tales like this one tried to explain the natural world without the aid of the scientific knowledge we have today.

Give each child **Copymaster 14 The story of Prometheus** and read it through with the children. This story deals with the beginning of creation by the Greek gods, of whom Prometheus was one.

- What natural phenomenon is the legend explaining?
- What elements in the story identify it as a traditional tale?

- What do they think of Prometheus' crime and punishment?
- Why would people think that fire was a supernatural thing?

The Origin of Fire

 Copymaster 15 The origin of fire is another ancient tale, this time from the legends of the Native American Indian, which seeks to explain how mankind came to be in possession of fire.

In groups, the children should read the story and discuss:

- any similarities and differences between this explanation and that of 'The story of Prometheus'
- any other explanations which the story seeks to give, for example the mark on the ground squirrel, the fact that the frog has no tail and that rubbing two sticks together can produce fire.

Summary

 Investigate the children's findings through class discussion and explore why they think many tales deal with the explanation of fire.

Session 2 ③

Introduction ⌊10-15 min⌋

Recap briefly on the type of traditional tale which the children have been reading, i.e. tales which seek to explain a natural phenomenon.

Explain that they are now going to write their own tale to explain one of the following:

- an eclipse of the sun
- a hurricane
- snow.

The children should work individually on this but a brainstorming class session prior to their planning and writing may prove useful. **Copymaster 16 Explaining** will give the children a framework for their planning.

Writing a legend to explain

Be on hand while the children are planning their tales to discuss the structure with them and to lead them into thinking laterally about what their chosen phenomenon could be mistaken for, e.g.

an eclipse:

- the sun is a god who, for some reason, has briefly turned his back on the Earth
- the sun and moon quarrelling about which one is the strongest
- many ancient peoples thought that a dragon had swallowed the sun and prayed during the eclipse for the dragon to spit it out again.

a hurricane:

- an angry god shouting
- one god being chased across the earth by another
- the gods having a race and breathing heavily.

snow:

- a god's dandruff
- the upturning of a giant salt pot.

Encourage the children to work in draft first, checking paragraphing, vivid description and detailing a logical, if somewhat far-fetched, explanation for the phenomenon.

The story of Prometheus

At the time of the creation, after covering the new-born Earth with luxuriant vegetation, and peopling it with living creatures of all kinds, the god Eros thought it was necessary to give all the creatures certain gifts so that they could enjoy life.

He called Prometheus and Epimetheus, the youngest sons of Lapetus to help him. They were to distribute gifts to the animals and to create a superior creature called Man who would rule over all the other creatures.

Prometheus and Epimetheus decided that they would give out gifts to the creatures that were already created and leave the creation of Man until the end. They were so generous that soon all the gifts and favours they had to give had been used up and there were none left to give to Man. They obeyed the god Eros and created the superior being called Man from clay and asked Eros to breathe life into the clay model.

Prometheus was especially pleased with what they had created and was troubled that he had no great gift to give to Man. He wanted something really special that would bring Man nearer to the gods than the other living creatures and he decided that his creation should have the gift of fire. This was, however, the special possession of the gods and Prometheus knew they would never share it with a mere mortal.

He thought long and hard about the problem and decided that the only way he could give fire to Man was to steal it from the gods, even though he knew he would never be forgiven and probably horribly punished if he were caught.

One night, after dark, Prometheus made his way to Mount Olympus, the home of the gods, stole a burning brand and escaped unseen. He was delighted his plan had worked so well and hurried to give the precious gift of fire to Man.

What Prometheus had done, however, was soon discovered! Jupiter, the king of the gods, was sitting on his throne on Mount Olympus when he saw an unusual light on the Earth below. It did not take him long to realise that the light was that of fire and that Prometheus was the thief.

So great was his fury that he seized Prometheus and bound him to a great rock in the Caucasian Mountains. But worse was to come. Jupiter ordered a fierce vulture to feast upon the liver of the unhappy Prometheus during the day. Each night, while Prometheus slept, his liver grew back only to be attacked and eaten again the next day.

After many centuries of such horrible torture, Jupiter's son Heracles found Prometheus, killed the vulture and set free the long-suffering god who had given such a wonderful gift to mankind.

Based on 'The story of Prometheus' from *Greece and Rome – Myths and Legends* by
H.A. Guerber

The origin of fire

The Karok had plenty of food, but there was no fire to cook it with. Far away, toward the rising sun, somewhere in a land which no Karok had ever seen, Kareya had made fire and hidden it in a casket, which he gave to two old hags to keep, lest some Karok should steal it. So now the coyote befriended the Karok, and promised to bring them some fire.

He went out and got together a great company of animals of every kind, from the lion down to the frog. These he stationed in a line all along the road from the home of the Karok to the far-distant land where the fire was, the weakest animal nearest home and the strongest near the fire. Then he took an Indian with him and hid him under a hill, and went to the cabin of the hags who kept the casket, and rapped on the door. One of them came out, and he said, 'Good evening,' and they replied, 'Good evening.' Then he said, 'it's a pretty cold night; can you let me sit by your fire?' And they said, 'Yes, come in.' So he went in and stretched himself out before the fire, and reached his snout out toward the blaze, and sniffed the heat and felt very snug and comfortable. Finally he stretched his nose out along his fore paws, and pretended to go to sleep, though he kept the corner of one eye open watching the old hags. But they never slept day or night, and he spent the whole night watching and thinking to no purpose.

So next morning he went out and told the Indian, whom he had hidden under the hill, that he must make an attack on the hags' cabin, as if he were about to steal some fire, while he (the coyote) was in it. He then went back and asked the hags to let him in again, which they did, as they did not think a coyote would steal any fire. He stood close by the casket of fire, and when the Indian made a rush on the cabin, and the hags dashed out after him at one door, the coyote seized a brand in his teeth and ran out at the other door. He almost flew over the ground; but the hags saw the sparks flying and gave chase, and gained on him fast. But by the time he was out of breath he reached the lion, who took the brand and ran with it to the next animal, and so on, each animal barely having time to give it to the next before the hags came up.

The next to the last in line was the ground squirrel. He took the brand and ran so fast with it that his tail got afire, and he curled it up over his back, and so burned the black spot we see to this day just behind his fore-shoulders. Last of all was the frog, but he, poor brute! couldn't run at all, so he opened his mouth wide and the squirrel chucked the fire into it, and he swallowed it down with a gulp. Then he turned and gave a great jump, but the hags were so close in pursuit that one of them seized him by the tail (he was a tadpole then) and tweaked it off, and that is the reason why frogs have no tails to this day. He swam under water a long distance, as long as he could hold his breath, then came up and spit out the fire into a log of driftwood, and there it has stayed safe ever since, so that when an Indian rubs two pieces of wood together the fire comes forth.

From *Classic Folk Tales from Around the World* introduced by Robert Nye

16 | Explaining

1 Explain one of the following (circle the one you choose):
- an eclipse of the sun
- a hurricane
- snow

2 Think about the characters in your story.
- Are they all men and women? _____
- What are their names? _____

_____

_____

- Are some of the characters gods and goddesses? _____
- What are their names and what powers do they have? _____

_____

_____

_____

3 Think about the setting.
- Where is your story going to take place? _____

_____

_____

_____

4 Think about what you are trying to explain.
- What could ancient people have thought was happening when they saw an eclipse of the sun, a hurricane or snow for the first time?

_____

_____

_____

_____

_____

Poetic forms

Learning targets

On completion of this unit the children should be able to:

1 ➤➤ read a range of narrative poems

2 ➤➤ understand terms which describe different kinds of poems, e.g. ballad, sonnet, rap, elegy, narrative poem, and to identify typical features

3 ➤➤ use the structures of poems read to write extensions based on these, e.g. additional verses, or substituting own words and ideas.

Before you start

Background knowledge

The three sessions in this unit deal with different kinds of poetic forms. It is by no means comprehensive, but will provide a structure for work on poetic forms which can be adapted to suit other groups of poems. The sessions can be spaced out in the term or can follow consecutively. Below are some 'technical' notes on the various forms:

Narrative poetry

A wide term used for any poem which essentially 'tells a story'. Structure and rhyme scheme vary and there is no set format.

Ballads

A form of narrative poetry falling into three main categories:

- popular ballad (also known as folk or traditional ballad) is a song which tells a story and is transmitted by word of mouth. The narrator is not involved in the story and expresses no personal feelings about it. These ballads take the listener straight into the story through describing action and using dialogue, and are traditionally written in 4 line verses – a quatrain – known as the ballad stanza. Whilst most popular ballads have their origin in Britain, there are also many American and Australian examples.

- broadside ballad is a type of ballad dating from the sixteenth century which was concerned with a current event sung to a popular tune. They were printed on one side of a sheet of paper called a broadside and were sold in the street or at gatherings such as country fairs.

- literary ballads are ballads written by established poets. They imitated the form of the traditional ballad but, unlike them, were not meant to be sung.

Sonnet

Sonnets are single stanza poems of 14 lines, usually with an intricate rhyme scheme. The subject matter of the sonnet was traditionally secular love but was extended by John Donne into a variety of religious themes.

- the Italian sonnet (also known as the Petrachan sonnet after the fourteenth-century Italian poet Petrach) falls into two main parts: the octet (8 lines) rhyming a b b a a b b a the sextet (6 lines) rhyming c d e c d e

- the English or Shakespearean sonnet was introduced in England in the sixteenth century and varied from the Italian sonnet by being composed of three quatrains (4 lines) rhyming a b a b/c d c d/e f e f with a concluding couplet g g.

Resources for Session 1

Copymaster 17 Jim

Resources for Session 2

Copymaster 18 The Rime of the Ancient Mariner

Resources for Session 3

Copymaster 19 There was an Indian
Copymaster 20 Ozymandias
Copymaster 21 The Vixen

Links to other units

Learning Targets: Reading and Writing Key Stage 1
Section 1 Units 1 to 6: Poetry
Learning Targets: Fiction and Poetry Years 3 and 4
Year 3 Term 1 Unit 3: Poetry writing
Year 4 Term 1 Unit 3: Poetry writing
Year 4 Term 2 Unit 2: Poems from long ago
Year 4 Term 3 Unit 2: Poetry forms
Year 4 Term 3 Unit 3: Syllabic poetry

Assessment indicators

- Can the children read and discuss various forms of poetry?
- Can they model their own poetry writing on poems read, including common features where appropriate?

Teaching the sessions

Session 1

Introduction   [20-30min]

▓ Begin by recapping on the forms of poetry which the children have met (see Links to other units).

As this session is essentially revisiting narrative poetry from Key Stage 1, ensure the children can define a narrative poem as one which tells a story.

Give each child **Copymaster 17 Jim**, and explain that, as well as being a narrative poem, this is an example of a cautionary tale. Define the term 'cautionary' by investigating the terms 'caution'/'being given a caution' so that the children understand that this type of poem issues a warning or teaches a lesson through a story. Explain that Belloc lived and wrote at the turn of the century and is most famous for his *Cautionary Tales* published in 1907.

Read through the poem with the children and discuss their immediate reaction.

*   What is the warning in the poem?
*   Do the children find it funny, sad, tragic?
*   How do they think the poet wanted them to feel?

To emphasise the 'narrative' aspect of the poem, link it to the elements in stories with which they are familiar:

*   plot
*   setting
*   character.

While the rhyme scheme in the poem is regular (a b a b) the verse form and the layout on the page is not. Do the children think that breaking up the structure of the poem with half lines and one word lines adds to the impact of the poem?

Investigate the capitalisation which contradicts much of what the children have been taught. Ask individual children to read a few lines and they will find themselves emphasising the words with capitals, i.e. the important words in each line.

A radio broadcast   [30min]

⁂ In groups, the children can prepare a reading of the poem as if it were being broadcast on the radio. Much of the poem is read by the narrator, so this part should be divided amongst several children in the group, along with the parts of Jim, the Keeper and Mother.

As the children are practising, discuss the intonation of the different speakers.

*   How would Jim shout 'Hi' when the lion was eating him?
*   How would the Keeper order Ponto to put Jim down?
*   How should various parts of the narrative be read? Should there be a difference in tone between the first 9 lines of the first verse and the last two?

Introduce the idea of 'pace' when reading poetry aloud. Will all of the poem be read at the same speed or will some parts of the story be quicker, e.g. when the lion sprang, and some parts slower, e.g. when the lion stops eating?

Summary   [10-20min]

▓ Allow some time for each group to practise and perform their rendition of the poem. Alternatively, give some groups other cautionary tales by Belloc to provide a variety of performances.

What happened next?   [30min]

 Although cautionary tales finish with the lesson that has to be learnt, explore what might have happened next to give the children a continuing story line on which to base an extension of the poem.

*   Did Father dismiss the Nurse?
*   Did the Keeper come round to apologise?
*   Was Ponto sent to another zoo?

Maintaining the a b a b rhyme scheme, can the children add some more lines to the sorry tale of Jim?

Homework

The children can choose one of the following for homework:

*   complete a neat, illustrated copy of their additional verses
*   retell the story of Jim in prose
*   retell the story of Jim as a front page newspaper report.

Session 2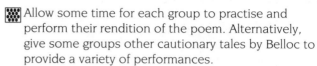

Introduction   [15-20min]

▓ Explain to the children that you are going to look at another form of narrative poem called a ballad.

Give the children **Copymaster 18 The Rime of the Ancient Mariner**, which is part 1 of the poem.

Read the poem to the children and to establish literal understanding, discuss the plot, characters and setting of the story so far. Investigate the words and phrases Coleridge uses to describe the various types of weather which the ship encountered.

Ensure the children understand that the Albatross was viewed as good luck by the sailors and to shoot it was an unforgivable crime. Discuss superstitions with which the children are familiar, e.g. walking under a ladder, breaking a mirror, a black cat crossing your path or spilling salt so that they appreciate that the sailors would expect bad luck on the rest of their journey.

What happened next?   [15-20min]

⁂ In groups, the children should discuss what they think happened to the ship. Stress that the sailor who shot the Albatross was not harmed in any way by the rest of the crew to avoid a predictably violent ending!

At this point the children should not be attempting to write verse but should be discussing possible story lines.

Summary

10-15 min

Discuss the story lines which the groups have come up with. The most popular one will probably be that the ship sank, so lead the children into considering other possibilities, e.g. lack of wind/becalmed, the crew struck down by some mysterious illness, the ship blown off course to the shore of a forbidding and inhospitable island.

Extending the poem

30 min

The children should choose a 'bad luck' scenario from their group and class discussions and add more four line verses to the poem, maintaining the a b a b rhyme scheme.

Homework

Make time to read the rest of the poem to the class as it provides various possibilities for individual writing. For example:

- Imagine you are the Ancient Mariner and write a letter to a close friend telling them what has happened.
- Make up a myth to explain why sailors looked upon the albatross as a lucky bird.

Session 3

 ② ③

Introduction

25-30 min

Defining a sonnet is complex as there have been many variations since its introduction as a poetic form in the fourteenth century. For the purposes of investigating this form with Y5-6/P6-7 children, it is sufficient to appreciate the common features of the 14 lines in which the first 8 lines (the octet) introduces the subject or theme, and the last 6 lines (the sextet) brings it to some sort of conclusion and provides a contrast in action or description.

Give each child **Copymaster 19 There was an Indian**. Read it through and discuss:

- what picture the poem presents in the first 8 lines, i.e. the Indian, peaceful and untroubled, gathering shells along the beach when he sees 'huge canoes'
- what picture the poem presents in the last 6 lines, i.e. the same Indian crouching in fear at a sight he does not understand
- what we are told about the Indian in each part of the poem:

octet	sextet
had known no change	in fear
strayed content	this naked man alone
gathering shells	lips gone pale
	knelt low
	did not understand

- the contrast between the octet and the sextet
- the use of description: 'huge canoes' (ships), 'bellying cloths on poles' (sails), 'fluttering coloured signs' (flags)
- what clue the word 'Columbus' gives about the poem (discovery of America in 1492 by Christopher Columbus)
- what the children think about this poem
- how they feel about the Indian
- how they feel about the seamen who land there
- what the children think the poet is saying by describing the ships as 'doom-burdened'

Sonnets

20 min

Copymaster 20 Ozymandias and **Copymaster 21 The Vixen** can provide the basis for group discussion. Each copymaster allows the children to discuss and make notes on the way the subject matter is treated in the octet and sextet.

- Ozymandias
  octet: a traveller describes the mysterious broken statue in the desert with its cruel, sneering face.
  sextet: the reader discovers the identity of the statue – Ozymandias, a powerful king in life, now a 'colossal wreck'.
- The Vixen
  octet: a vivid description of a fox playing with her cubs. Always alert to any danger, protecting her cubs by ensuring they go to ground when danger threatens.
  sextet: a shepherd's boy pokes the foxes' hole with a stick, he fails to harm them and, when danger has passed, they come out to play again.

Summary

10-15 min

Investigate the children's findings through class discussion, ensuring there is time for them to express their feelings about the poems.

Writing a sonnet

30 min

Depending on how well you think the children can cope with writing a sonnet, this can be an individual, pair or group activity.

Alternatively, this can be a whole class task.

- Agree on a subject or theme where a change or contrast is evident, e.g.

octet	sextet
description of forest →	forest on fire
storm clouds building →	the storm
a long, tiring journey →	arrival

- the children can suggest opening lines and all should contribute to the construction of the poem.

It adds an unnecessary complication to agree on or impose a rhyme scheme from the outset. See how the work in progress is evolving and edit and modify lines to introduce an element of rhyme. Guide the children, if possible, away from simply having 7 rhyming couplets of a b a b, towards something more sophisticated.

Jim

Jim, who ran away from his Nurse, and was eaten by a Lion.

There was a Boy whose name was Jim;
His Friends were very good to him.
They gave him Tea, and Cakes, and Jam,
And slices of delicious Ham,
And Chocolate with pink inside,
And little Tricycles to ride,
And read him Stories through and through,
And even took him to the Zoo –
But there it was the dreadful Fate
Befell him, which I now relate.

You know – at least you *ought* to know,
For I have often told you so –
That Children never are allowed
To leave their Nurses in a crowd;
Now this was Jim's especial Foible,
He ran away when he was able,
And on this inauspicious day
He slipped his hand and ran away!
He hadn't gone a yard when –
                  Bang!

With open Jaws, a Lion sprang,
And hungrily began to eat
The Boy: beginning at his feet.

Now just imagine how it feels
When first your toes and then your heels,
And then by gradual degrees,
Your shins and ankles, calves and knees,
Are slowly eaten, bit by bit.

No wonder Jim detested it!
No wonder that he shouted 'Hi!'
The Honest Keeper heard his cry,
Though very fat
          he almost ran
To help the little gentleman.
'Ponto!' he ordered as he came
(For Ponto was the Lion's name),
'Ponto!' he cried,
         with angry Frown.
'Let go, Sir! Down, Sir! Put it down!'

The Lion made a sudden Stop,
He let the Dainty Morsel drop,
And slunk reluctant to his Cage,
Snarling with Disappointed Rage
But when he bent him over Jim,
The Honest Keeper's
         Eyes were dim.
The lion having reached his Head,
The Miserable Boy was dead!

When Nurse informed his Parents, they
Were more Concerned than I can say: –
His Mother, as She dried her eyes,
Said, 'Well – it gives me no surprise,
He would not do as he was told!'
His father, who was self-controlled,
Bade all the children round attend
To James' miserable end,
And always keep a-hold of Nurse
For fear of finding something worse

Hilaire Belloc

Part 1

It is an ancient Mariner
And he stoppeth one of three.
'By thy long grey beard and glittering eye,
Now wherefore stopp'st thou me?

An ancient Mariner
meeteth three Gallants
bidden to a wedding-feast,
and detaineth one.

The Bridegroom's doors are opened wide,
And I am next of kin;
The guests are met, the feast is set:
Mayst hear the merry din.'

He holds him with his skinny hand,
'There was a ship,' quoth he.
'Hold off! unhand me, grey-beard loom!'
Eftsoons his hand dropt he.

He holds him with his glittering eye –
The Wedding-Guest stood still,
And listens like a three years' child:
The Mariner hath his will.

The Wedding-Guest is spellbound
by the eye of the old
seafaring man, and constrained
to hear his tale.

The Wedding-Guest sat on a stone:
He cannot choose but hear;
And thus spake on that ancient man,
The bright-eyed Mariner.

'The ship was cheered, the harbour cleared,
Merrily did we drop
Below the kirk, below the hill,
Below the lighthouse top.

The Mariner tells how the ship
sailed southward with a good
wind and fair weather, till it
reached the Line.

The Sun came up upon the left,
Out of the sea came he!
And he shone bright, and on the right
Went down into the sea.

Higher and higher every day,
Till over the mast at noon –'
The Wedding-Guest here beat his breast,
For he heard the loud bassoon.

The bride hath paced into the hall,
Red as a rose is she;
Nodding their heads before her goes
The merry minstrelsy.

The Wedding-Guest heareth the
bridal music; but the Mariner
continueth his tale.

The Wedding-Guest he beat his breast,
Yet he cannot choose but hear;
And thus spake on that ancient man,
The bright-eyed Mariner.

The Rime of the Ancient Mariner
(cont.)

'And now the STORM-BLAST came, and he
Was tyrannous and strong:
He struck with his o'ertaking wings,
And chased us south along.

The ship driven by a storm towards the South Pole.

With sloping masts and dipping prow,
As who pursued with yell and blow
Still treads the shadow of his foe,
And forward bends his head,
The ship drove fast, loud roared the blast,
And southward aye we fled.

And now there came both mist and snow,
And it grew wondrous cold:
And ice, mast-high, came floating by,
As green as emerald.

And through the drifts the snowy clifts
Did send a dismal sheen:
Nor shapes of men nor beasts we ken –
The ice was all between.

The land of ice, and of fearful sounds, where no living thing was to be seen.

The ice was here, the ice was there,
The ice was all around:
It cracked and growled, and roared and howled,
Like noises in a swound!

At length did cross an Albatross,
Thorough the fog it came:
As if it had been a Christian soul,
We hailed it in God's name.

Till a great sea-bird, called the Albatross, came through the snow-fog, and was received with great joy and hospitality.

It ate the food it ne'er had eat,
And round and round it flew.
The ice did split with a thunder-fit;
The helmsman steered us through!

And a good south wind sprung up behind;
The Albatross did follow,
And every day, for food or play,
Came to the mariners' hollo!

And lo! the Albatross proveth a bird of good omen, and followeth the ship as it returned northward through fog and floating ice.

In mist or cloud, on mast or shroud,
It perched for vespers nine;
Whiles all the night, through fog-smoke white,
Glimmered the white Moon-shine.'

'God save thee, ancient Mariner!
From the fiends, that plague thee thus! –
Why look'st thou so?' – 'With my cross-bow
I shot the ALBATROSS.'

The ancient Mariner inhospitably killeth the pious bird of good omen.

Samuel Taylor Coleridge

There was an Indian

There was an Indian, who had known no change,
   Who strayed content along a sunlit beach
Gathering shells. He heard a sudden strange
   Commingled noise; looked up; and gasped for speech
For in the bay, where nothing was before,
   Moved on the sea, by magic, huge canoes,
With bellying cloths on poles, and not one oar,
   And fluttering coloured signs and clambering crews.
And he, in fear, this naked man alone,
   His fallen hands forgetting all their shells,
His lips gone pale, knelt low behind a stone,
   And stared, and saw, and did not understand,
Columbus's doom-burdened caravels
   Slant to the shore, and all their seamen land.

Sir John Squire

I met a traveller from an antique land
Who said: Two vast and trunkless legs of stone
Stand in the desert. Near them, on the sand,
Half sunk, a shatter'd visage lies, whose frown,
And wrinkled lip, and sneer of cold command,
Tell that its sculptor well those passions read
Which yet survive, stamp'd on these lifeless things.
The hand that mock'd them and the heart that fed:
And on the pedestal these words appear:
'My name is Ozymandias, king of kings:
Look on my works, ye Mighty, and despair!'
Nothing beside remains. Round the decay
Of that colossal wreck, boundless and bare
The lone and level sands stretch far away.

Percy Bysshe Shelley

Make notes on what is being described in:

the octet

_____

_____

_____

_____

_____

_____

_____

the sextet

_____

_____

_____

_____

_____

_____

_____

The Vixen

Among the taller wood with ivy hung,
The old fox plays and dances round her young.
She snuffs and barks if any passes by
And swings her tail and turns prepared to fly.
The horseman hurries by, she bolts to see,
And turns agen, from danger never free.
If any stands she runs among the poles
And barks and snaps and drives them in their holes.
The shepherd sees them and the boy goes by
And gets a stick and progs the hole to try.
They get all still and lie in safety sure,
And out again when everything's secure,
And start and snap at blackbirds bouncing by
To fight and catch the great white butterfly.

John Clare

Make notes on what is being described in:

the octet   the sextet

_____   _____

_____   _____

_____   _____

_____   _____

_____   _____

_____   _____

UNIT 3 | Science fiction

Learning targets

On completion of this unit the children should be able to:

1 ➡➤ investigate the features of different fiction genres, e.g. science fiction, adventure, discussing the appeal of popular fiction

2 ➡➤ review and edit writing to produce a final form, matched to the needs of an identified reader.

Before you start

Background knowledge

The reading objective on which these sessions are based is ambitious because it demands a wide range of reading for the children and a considerable amount of time for them to be familiar enough with any given genre to be able to evaluate it.

This unit on science fiction is a model on which work on other genres can be based, and is, perhaps, the easiest to tackle in extract form, drawing on the children's experience of television and film portrayal of the genre. It is also the most interesting as it offers the unusual dimension of a literary form which changes. Science *fiction* can become science *fact*, and innovative science fiction can become a *historical* narrative, depending on when it is written and when it is read.

The three sessions explore this dimension along with the common features of the genre.

Resources for Session 1

Copymaster 22 A short history of space travel
Copymaster 23 The War of the Worlds

Resources for Session 2

Copymaster 24 Who's There?

Resources for Session 3

Copymaster 25 Apollo 13

Assessment indicators

- Can the children recognise science fiction as a genre?
- Can they appreciate how science fiction can become science fact?
- Can they produce a science fiction story?

Teaching the sessions

Session 1 ❶

Introduction   20-25 min

▨ Begin by ascertaining what the children understand by the term 'science fiction'. Ask for examples (most of which will probably come from television and film) and through discussion define the term:

'fiction based on imagined future scientific or technological advances, major social or environmental changes, etc. frequently portraying space or time travel, life on other planets, etc.'

(*Concise Oxford Dictionary*)

Ask the children to help you compile a list on the board of possible ingredients for a science fiction story, e.g.

- visiting other planets
- aliens visiting our planet
- fantastic machines which can travel through space and time.

With the aid of **Copymaster 22 A short history of space travel** look at the history of man's attempts to conquer space in order to give the children a time scale against which to judge the various extracts. Some enthusiasts in the class may be able to add more detail or extend the information given to include further Apollo missions or the unmanned Voyager spacecraft which explored the giant planets at the limits of our solar system.

Having given the children some insight into man's space explorations, give each child **Copymaster 23 The War of the Worlds**. Explain that this was written in 1898. Read it through with the children and discuss it in terms of science fiction, science fact and historical narration. In this instance, the passing of about a hundred years has not changed what was, and is, a science fiction story.

Evaluation　|20-25 min|

The children should work in groups to discuss the extract in terms of:

- its appeal to the reader – why would people enjoy/dislike this kind of story?
- its credibility – is it believable? Does its credibility/incredibility affect the reader's enjoyment?
- the quality of the writing – is Wells' description of the Martian effective? Is it detailed enough? Is it too detailed?
- the narrative viewpoint – does it help the reader to have the story told as a first person narrative? Would it have been more or less effective as a third person narrative?

Summary　|10-15 min|

Explore the children's conclusions through class discussion. If time permits, extend the work on this extract by playing part 2 of Jeff Wayne's Musical Version of *The War of the Worlds*: 'Horsell Common and the Heat Ray' (1978 CBS Records). This will provide an interesting comparison between the original story and a much later musical/narrative interpretation.

Session 2　①　②

Introduction　|10-15 min|

This session is based on the first part of a short story by Arthur C. Clarke which was first published in 1958. At the time it was published it was a science *fiction* story, but there is much in it that is now *fact*, e.g. walking on the moon, space suits, satellites, space stations – albeit not the sophisticated structure being built in the story.

You can either follow the structure of the first session and read and discuss **Copymaster 24 Who's There?** with the children. Alternatively, the children can work in groups to discuss the extract without initial guidance.

Evaluation　|15-20 min|

The children should discuss:
- when they think the story was written?
- what categorises it as a science fiction story?
- in what ways is it similar/different to the extract from *The War of the Worlds*?

Summary　|10-15 min|

Explore the children's findings through class discussion.

- Did they appreciate that to be science *fiction*, the story must have been written some time ago?
- Comparison with *The War of the Worlds*:
  Similarities: very detailed, involves space travel, first person narrative
  Differences: man has left the Earth as opposed to aliens coming to Earth

Of the two extracts, which do the children consider is still science *fiction* and which do they consider has moved into the realm of science *fact*?

How does it end?　|30 min|

The narrator of the story has left the space station to get the satellite. What happens next? The children should write a science fiction ending for the story.

Session 3　①　②

Introduction　|15 min|

Copymaster 25 Apollo 13, moves the genre into the realms of historical narrative with the story of the near disastrous mission to the moon in Apollo 13. What, many years ago, would have been the stuff of science fiction, is today a story based on actual historical events.

Explain to the children that Apollo 13 never made it to the moon because one of the fuel tanks exploded and the three crew members were lucky to make it back to Earth alive.

Read the opening chapter with the children and ask them to put themselves in the place of:
- Neil Armstrong: What would it have felt like to be the first to step on to the moon's surface?
- Buzz Aldrin: What would it have felt like to be the *second* man on the moon?
- Remind them of the **Copymaster 22 A short history of space travel**. What part did Michael Collins play in the moon landing? How would they have felt if they were Michael Collins?
- Can they understand how desperately Jim Lovell wanted to walk on the moon? Would they like to walk on the moon?

A science fiction story　|30 min|

The children can choose to write a detailed description of either an alien visiting Earth, modelled on *The War of the Worlds* or a crew of astronauts visiting an imaginary planet, modelled on *Who's There?* and *Apollo 13*.

Stress that detailed descriptions will make their stories more credible and that they should avoid clichéd encounters with 'bug-eyed monsters' who immediately 'zap' with their ray guns!

A short history of space travel

1957　　The USSR launched Sputnik 2 carrying a dog named Laika. The dog was the first living creature in space.

April 1961　Yuri Gagarin flew in the USSR spacecraft Vostok 1. He was the first human in space.

May 1961　The USA launched a Mercury spacecraft piloted by Alan Shepard, the first American in space.

Aug 1961　Vostok 2, piloted by Gherman Titov, orbited the Earth.

Feb 1962　A Mercury spacecraft, piloted by John Glenn, orbited the Earth.

Aug 1962　Vostok 3 with Andrian Nikolayev and Vostock 4 with Pavel Popovich passed within 3 miles of each other in space.

June 1963　Vostock 5 launched the first woman, Valentina Tereshkova into space.

Mar 1965　The USSR's Voskhod spacecraft had Alexei Leonov aboard. He became the first man to walk in space.

June 1965　America's Edward White took his space walk from Gemini 4.

Dec 1968　Frank Borman, Jim Lovell and Bill Anders were the first astronauts to orbit the moon in Apollo 8

July 1969　Apollo 11 orbited the moon. From it, Neil Armstrong and Buzz Aldrin piloted the Lunar Module 'Eagle' on to the moon's surface. Neil Armstrong was the first man to set foot on the moon, closely followed by Buzz Aldrin. Michael Collins, the third crew member, continued to orbit the moon until the lunar mission was completed and his fellow astronauts returned to Apollo 11.

The War of the Worlds

At the beginning of the book, the narrator tells of flares of what look like gas and flames squirting out of the planet Mars. Shortly afterwards, what appeared to be falling stars were seen in the sky but when they fell to Earth they were discovered to be large metal cylinders. One fell on Horsell Common, not far from the narrator's home and he went to see what it was all about.

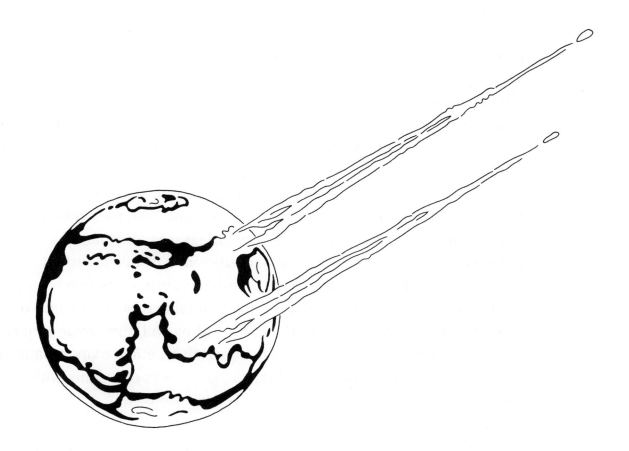

The end of the cylinder was being screwed out from within. Nearly two feet of shining screw projected. Somebody blundered against me, and I narrowly missed being pitched on to the top of the screw. I turned, and as I did so the screw must have come out, and the lid of the cylinder fell upon the gravel with a ringing concussion. I stuck my elbow into the person behind me, and turned my head towards the thing again. For a moment that circular cavity seemed perfectly black. I had the sunset in my eyes.

I think everyone expected to see a man emerge – possibly something a little unlike us terrestrial men, but in all essentials a man. I know I did. But, looking, I presently saw something stirring within the shadow – greyish billowy movements, one above another, and then two luminous discs like eyes. Then something resembling a little grey snake, about the thickness of a walking-stick, coiled up out of the writhing middle, and wriggled in the air towards me – and then another.

A sudden chill came over me. There was a loud shriek from a woman behind. I half turned, keeping my eyes fixed upon the cylinder still, from which other tentacles were now projecting, and began pushing my way back from the edge of the pit. I saw astonishment giving place to horror on the faces of the people about me …

A big greyish, rounded bulk, the size perhaps, of a bear, was rising slowly and painfully out of the cylinder. As it bulged up and caught the light, it glistened like wet leather. Two large dark-coloured eyes were regarding me steadfastly. It was rounded, and had, one might say, a face. There was a mouth under the eyes, the brim of which quivered and panted, and dropped saliva. The body heaved and pulsated convulsively. A lank tentacular appendage gripped the edge of the cylinder, another swayed in the air.

Those who have never seen a living Martian can scarcely imagine the strange horror of their appearance. The peculiar V-shaped mouth with its pointed upper lip, the absence of brow ridges, the absence of a chin beneath the wedge-like lower lip, the incessant quivering of this mouth, the Gorgon group of tentacles, the tumultuous breathing of the lungs in a strange atmosphere, the evident heaviness and painfulness of movement, due to the greater gravitational energy of the earth – above all, the extraordinary intensity of the immense eyes – culminated in an effect akin to nausea … Even at this first encounter, this first glimpse, I was overcome with disgust and dread.

Suddenly the monster vanished.

From *The War of the Worlds* by H.G. Wells

Who's there?

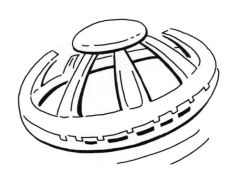

When Satellite Control called me, I was writing up the day's progress report in the Observation Bubble – the glass-domed office that juts out from the axis of the Space Station like the hubcap of a wheel. It was not really a good place to work, for the view was too overwhelming. Only a few yards away I could see the construction teams performing their slow-motion ballet as they put the station together like a giant jigsaw puzzle. And beyond them, twenty thousand miles below, was the blue-green glory of the full Earth, floating against the ravelled star clouds of the Milky Way.

'Station Supervisor here,' I answered. 'What's the trouble?'

'Our radar's showing a small echo two miles away, almost stationary, about five degrees west of Sirius. Can you give us a visual report on it?'

Anything matching our orbit so precisely could hardly be a meteor; it would have to be something we'd dropped – perhaps an inadequately secured piece of equipment that had drifted away from the station. So I assumed; but when I pulled out my binoculars and searched the sky around Orion, I soon found my mistake. Though this space traveller was man-made, it had nothing to do with us.

'I've found it,' I told Control. 'It's someone's test satellite – cone-shaped, four antennae, and what looks like a lens system at its base. Probably U.S. Air Force, early nineteen-sixties, judging by the design. I know they lost track of several when their transmitters failed. There were quite a few attempts to hit this orbit before they finally made it.'

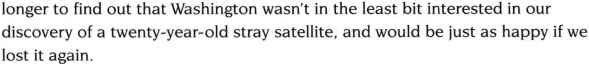

After a brief search through the files, Control was able to confirm my guess. It took a little longer to find out that Washington wasn't in the least bit interested in our discovery of a twenty-year-old stray satellite, and would be just as happy if we lost it again.

'Well, we can't do *that*,' said Control. 'Even if nobody wants it, the thing's a menace to navigation. Someone had better go out and haul it aboard.'

That someone, I realized, would have to be me. I dared not detach a man from the closely knit construction teams, for we were already behind schedule – and a single day's delay on this job cost a million dollars. All the radio and

Who's there? (cont.)

TV networks on Earth were waiting impatiently for the moment when they could route their programmes through us, and thus provide the first truly global service, spanning the world from Pole to Pole.

'I'll go out and get it,' I answered, snapping an elastic band over my papers so that the air currents from the ventilators wouldn't set them wandering around the room. Though I tried to sound as if I was doing everyone a great favour, I was secretly not at all displeased. It had been at least two weeks since I'd been outside; I was getting a little tired of stores schedules, maintenance reports, and all the glamorous ingredients of a Space Station Supervisor's life.

The only member of the staff I passed on my way to the air lock was Tommy, our recently acquired cat. Pets mean a great deal to men thousands of miles from Earth, but there are not many animals that can adapt themselves to a weightless environment. Tommy mewed plaintively at me as I clambered into my spacesuit, but I was in too much of a hurry to play with him.

At this point, perhaps I should remind you that the suits we use on the station are completely different from the flexible affairs men wear when they want to walk around on the moon. Ours are really baby spaceships, just big enough to hold one man. They are stubby cylinders, about seven feet long, fitted with low-powered propulsion jets, and have a pair of accordion-like sleeves at the upper end for the operator's arms. Normally, however, you keep your hands drawn inside the suit, working the manual controls in front of your chest.

As soon as I'd settled down inside my very exclusive spacecraft, I switched on power and checked the gauges on the tiny instrument panel. There's a magic word, 'FORB', that you'll often hear spacemen mutter as they climb into their suits; it reminds them to test fuel, oxygen, radio, batteries. All my needles were well in the safety zone, so I lowered the transparent hemisphere over my head and sealed myself in. For a short trip like this, I did not bother to check the suit's internal lockers, which were used to carry food and special equipment for extended missions.

As the conveyor belt decanted me into the air lock, I felt like an Indian papoose being carried along on its mother's back. Then the pumps brought the pressure down to zero, the outer door opened, and the last traces of air swept me out into the stars, turning very slowly head over heels.

From *Who's There?* by Arthur C. Clarke

Apollo 13

July 20, 1969

The rough, lonely surface of the moon had been waiting for a long, long time. Meteors may have brushed its dusty, craggy craters. Debris from the deepest regions of outer space may have pierced its dead exterior. But never before had life touched it. Not until now. Today, for the first time, footsteps would fall on the battered surface. Laughter would awaken its dead soul. For one tiny blink in the history of the universe, man would cast a shadow over the moon's lonely craters.

And then it happened. The astronaut Neil Armstrong, moved onto the top of the steps and looked around. He glanced down at the lunar surface, then turned and moved carefully down the ladder, grasping the railings with his bulky gloves. When he reached the bottom, he stopped.

As the world watched from their living rooms, the astronaut poised above the moon waited. The surface of the moon waited. And far away, seated in front of television sets back on Earth, Jim Lovell, Fred Haise, and Bill Anders, the Apollo 11 backup team, waited too. Each member of that team had hoped to be the first to step onto the moon. But it was not to be. They would not be first. But they knew that they would be there some day.

'Some day I'm going to take that step,' Jim Lovell said to his youngest son, Jeffrey. They were sitting on the couch, staring at the television screen. Across the room, Jim's wife Marilyn frowned. For Jim's sake, she hoped that his words would come true. But she also dreaded each and every space mission.

Jim's other children, fifteen-year-old Jay, fourteen-year-old Barbara, and eleven-year-old Susan moved closer to the television set.

And then, over 200,000 miles above them, Neil Armstrong took the first step on the moon.

'That was one small step for man, one giant step for mankind,' his voice crackled as it beamed through the universe to the people back home.

'Look at the rocks, Dad!' the five-year-old shouted. 'Look at the moon rocks!'

'I see them, Jeffrey,' Jim said, as the second astronaut emerged from the spacecraft. Buzz Aldrin stood at the top of the ladder for a second, then he too began to climb down.

'Are you really going to the moon?' Jeffrey turned to face his father. Jim Lovell had gone to the moon once before, but he had never walked on it. It had been the Apollo 8 mission, the first mission to circle the moon.

'It looks like it, Jeffrey,' Jim said. 'I'm told I'll be commanding the Apollo 14 mission to the moon. Pete Conrad will command the Apollo 12 mission. Then Alan Shepard will lead Apollo 13. And then it's my turn.'

'And will you bring me a moon rock?'

'If there is any way that I can, I will.'

'Do you promise?' Jeffrey asked.

Jim Lovell put his arm around his son.

Jim had been waiting for such a long time. But he knew that some day it would be his shadow passing over the moon.

'I promise,' Jim whispered. 'If there is any way at all, I will bring you a moon rock.'

From *Apollo 13 – The Junior Novelization* adapted by Dina Anastasio

Butterflies don't know much. This one didn't know it was a chequered skipper – one of only sixty left in the world. It didn't know that this sun-dappled clearing was part of Rockingham Forest, and it certainly didn't know that its quick, darting flight was closely observed by three humans, two of whom weren't even born yet.

Heavy with the eggs it bore, the insect alighted on a leaf. At once the surrounding air became suffused with a soft, pulsating glow. The leaf trembled for an instant ever so faintly and when it stopped, the butterfly had gone.

'There you go, folks.' Harper Rye held up the flask for her children to see. 'One chequered skipper, extinct for twenty years yet very much alive, undamaged and beautifully pregnant. We've finally cracked it, my darlings.'

'Oh, Mum!' Kizzy, a ten-year-old version of her mother with the same straight dark hair and glasses, flung her arms around Harper's neck and kissed her on the mouth. 'I knew you'd do it. I *always* knew.'

'Steady!' Harper set down the flask before returning the child's embrace. 'Of course you did, my precious. Your faith in your old mum has been positively unswerving.'

'I knew you'd do it too,' growled Frazer. At thirteen he was less demonstrative than his sister and more cynical. 'What I *didn't* know was that you'd get all excited over butterflies and stuff when you could be snatching people. I mean, why can't we bring *Granny* back or something?'

Harper's grin faded as she looked at her son. 'Because, my love, the ability to create new technology carries with it heavy responsibilities. If we were to misuse my invention it might cause untold harm. For example, to snatch a human being – any human being – could alter history in some dramatic way we haven't even dreamed of. No.' She shook her head. 'Rule one *must* be – no humans.'

Frazer raked a hand through his mop of ginger curls. 'Hmmm. Never thought of that, Mum. Altering history, I mean. So that's why we're sticking to animals and plants – because that won't change history?'

'It *will*', smiled Harper, 'but hopefully not in ways which will be harmful, or even particularly noticeable.'

Kizzy gazed at her mother's machine – a machine which could vanish and reappear like something in a magic show. It reminded her of an enormous doughnut. In fact, she'd christened it 'the Doughnut' without telling the other two. 'It's absolutely fantastic, Mum,' she breathed. 'What will you call it?'

'Oh – Rye's Apparatus, I expect. It's got a sort of ring to it, don't you think?'

Kizzy nodded. Better than the Doughnut, she thought.

'Rye's Apparatus.' Frazer rolled the words across his tongue a couple of times, then nodded. 'Ye-es. That sounds suitably historic, Ma – like Parkinson's Disease and Sod's Law. I reckon it'll do.'

Harper Rye laughed. 'I don't know about historic, my love. It might be best to keep this whole thing to ourselves, at least for the time being …

From *Timesnatch* by Robert Swindells

Timesnatch (2)

Read through the opening extract from *Timesnatch*.
- Summarise the story so far.
- Write what you think might happen next.

Your opinion
- Do you think you would like to read this book?
  Give your reasons.

- Do you think you would not like to read this book?
  Give your reasons

Science fiction
The concept of time travel is still science fiction as no one has been able to achieve it.

Imagine you are Kizzy or Frazer in the story and that you have used your mother's machine to bring someone famous back from the past.
- Who would it be?
- Write a story about what happens.

Traditional tales
Butterflies come in many different colours and with many different patterns.

Write a traditional tale to explain why, in the beginning, all butterflies were white and how they came to be so different.

YEAR 5 TERM 3

Focus

In this section the children will be given the opportunity to:

1 Investigate narrative perspective within the reading range of stories from other cultures
2 Read and perform performance poetry
3 Look closely at extracts around a common theme from Victorian literature.

Content

Unit 1: Narrative perspective
Unit 2: Performance poetry
Unit 3: Older literature

Extract list

Angelou, Maya: 'On Aging'
Brand, Dionne: 'Old Men of Magic'
Dickens, Charles: *Oliver Twist*
Kingsley, Charles: *The Water-babies*
Loeff, A Rutgers van der: *Avalanche!*
Smucker, Barbara: *Underground to Canada*

Assessment

Assessment Copymaster 40 is at the end of the section.

Copymaster 40 Points of view

Curriculum Planner
National Literacy Strategy Planner

This chart shows you how to find activities by unit to resource your term's requirements for text level work on fiction and poetry. The Learning Targets closely follow the structure of the fiction and poetry requirements for the term in the National Literacy Strategy document (pages 48–49). A few of the requirements are not covered.

YEAR 5 Term 3

Range

Fiction and poetry:

- novels, stories and poems from a variety of cultures and traditions
- choral and performance poetry.

TEXT LEVEL WORK

COMPREHENSION AND COMPOSITION

Reading comprehension

Pupils should be taught:

2 to identify the point of view from which a story is told and how this affects the reader's response; Unit 1

3 to change point of view, e.g. tell incident or describe a situation from the point of view of another character or perspective; Unit 1

4 to read, rehearse and modify performance of poetry; Unit 2

5 to select poetry, justify their choices, e.g. in compiling class anthology; Unit 2

6 to explore the challenge and appeal of older literature through:

- listening to older literature being read aloud;
- reading accessible poems, stories and extracts;
- reading extracts from classic serials shown on television;
- discussing differences in language used; Unit 3

Writing composition

Pupils should be taught:

7 to write from another character's point of view, e.g. retelling an incident in letter form; Unit 1

9 to write in the style of the author, e.g. writing on to complete a section, resolve a conflict; writing additional dialogue, new chapter; Unit 3

UNIT 1 Narrative perspective

Learning targets

On completion of this unit the children should be able to:

1 ➤➤ identify the point of view from which a story is told and how this affects the reader's response

2 ➤➤ change point of view, e.g. tell incident or describe a situation from the point of view of another character or perspective

3 ➤➤ write from another character's point of view, e.g. retelling an incident in letter form.

Before you start

Background knowledge

The two extracts in this unit are from a European culture and an American culture respectively.

Avalanche!
This story has a basis in fact because many Alpine villages face the threat of avalanches. It was first published in Holland in 1954 and was translated into English in 1957.

Underground to Canada
This story is set against the factual background of slave owning plantations in the southern states of America. The American Civil War was fought between the northern states which had abolished slavery and the southern states which maintained it was their right to own slaves. Many slaves made the tortuous journey north, aided by white abolitionists, to gain their freedom in Canada.

Resources for Session 1

Copymaster 28 Avalanche!
Copymaster 29 Analysing the text

Resources for Session 2

Copymaster 30 Underground to Canada
Copymaster 31 Changing the viewpoint

Links to other units

Learning Targets: Fiction and Poetry Years 3 and 4
Year 3 Term 3 Unit 2: First person accounts

Assessment indicators

- Can the children recognise how an author can:
  relate incidents in the story from his/her viewpoint
  allow a reader to see the viewpoint of one or more characters?
- Can they rewrite incidents from the viewpoint of one particular character?

Teaching the sessions

Session 1 ①

Introduction [20min]

▓ This unit combines texts from various cultures, focusing on narrative perspective, i.e. the point of view from which a story is told. As a starting point ask the children what they understand by the terms 'different cultures' and 'different traditions'.

Ensure the children appreciate that 'different cultures' can be found in parts of their own country as well as in countries all over the world. Although we consider ourselves to be Europeans, there are marked cultural contrasts between, for example, Britain and Spain, France and Germany, etc. The range of texts from different cultures should not be restricted to those that are considered to be from a

very different cultural background from our own. Interesting cultural comparisons can be made using texts that appear to be culturally very similar to our own.

What do the children understand by the term narrative perspective?

Most stories which the children encounter are told from the author's point of view and are written in the third person. Within this narrative perspective, however, certain episodes and incidents can be written from the point of view of one character or a group of characters. This device allows the reader to see how the characters respond to the events in the story.

The other common narrative perspective is that of a first person account where the story is told through the eyes of one particular character.

Discuss the advantages and disadvantages of each type of narrative perspective.

Avalanche! ⏱ 30 min

 Give each group **Copymaster 28 Avalanche!** and explain the cultural background of the story. (See Background knowledge.) The children should read and discuss the extract in terms of:

*   narrative perspective
*   character perspective.

They can use **Copymaster 29 Analysing the text** to record their findings. Be on hand to help with difficult vocabulary.

Summary ⏱ 15–20 min

▦ Discuss the children's conclusions.

This is a third person account, therefore the narrative perspective is that of the author. He does, however, allow the reader to appreciate that Bartel and the older villagers have different views of the situation.

Bartel
We get the impression that Bartel is not worried about the possibility of an avalanche:

*   he thinks the sun is breaking through
*   he thinks the two snow covered mountains look 'good and quiet'
*   he thinks the school children are lucky to get time off school because of the weather.

The older villagers
We get the impression that they are worried:

*   they 'stared anxiously up at the steep slopes'
*   they 'shook their heads anxiously, looking more worried every hour'
*   they recognise the warning signs – 'It was too mild for the time of year and the wind was changeable. Just like the year of disaster, 1927'
*   'their faces under their woollen scarves were pale and serious'.

John

*   'Bad, very bad'
*   'Children are children ... They don't know what's in store for them.'
*   'But the Kühelihorn and the Glarbeckscher will teach you something yet!'
*   'Oh, yes. Good and quiet. That's what you say'

Which viewpoint do the children agree with?

Which viewpoint do they think the author wants them to share?

Session 2 ② ③

Introduction ⏱ 20–25 min

▦ Remind the children that you are looking at the viewpoint from which a story is told and give out copies of **Copymaster 30 Underground to Canada**.

Ask the children what they know about the slave trade and slavery in America, ensuring they understand the cultural background against which this story is set. (See Background knowledge.)

Read through the extract and discuss the characters, the situation and the narrative perspective (the

perspective of the author) to ensure the children have understood the piece.

Changing the viewpoint ⏱ 20 min

 Put the children into groups of 4 or 5 and give each group one of the following characters to discuss:

*   Liza
*   Lester
*   Julilly
*   Adam
*   the wagon driver.

Copymaster 31 Changing the viewpoint is for the children to make notes on what they find out about a particular character from the extract, including details of what they say and do. This is in preparation for individual writing where they will rewrite the extract from that character's point of view.

Summary ⏱ 20 min

▦ Discuss each character in turn:

Liza

*   doesn't trust white men
*   thin and weak
*   bent-up back
*   wants to stay hidden for a long time
*   religious

Lester

*   the leader
*   will fight to protect them from slave catchers
*   determined to escape
*   can read
*   observant
*   worried about the slave catchers

Julilly

*   concerned about the others
*   would carry Liza if needed
*   brave
*   quick thinking

the wagon driver

*   knows the signal and password
*   brisk and small
*   taken Mr Ross's place
*   brave
*   quick to see what has to be done

A character's point of view ⏱ 30 min

🔲 The children can choose the character they have worked on in the group or one of the others. They should rewrite the episode from that character's point of view, taking into account what the character says and does but adding their thoughts and feelings and writing in the first person.

Homework

The children can choose another character and write the episode in the form of a letter to a close friend.

Avalanche!

On Monday January the seventeenth early in the morning it began to snow. It snowed and snowed, hour after hour, day and night. By Friday there were more than six feet of fresh snow on top of the old, hard-packed layer that had been lying there since December. And still it went on snowing.

But it seemed to be growing lighter. There was a change in the sky. By midday the snow had thinned to a few fluttering flakes, and for the first time for days one could see some distance.

The old people in the little mountain village of Urteli, now completely cut off by the snow, stared anxiously up at the steep slopes where the black patches of pine forest were now almost hidden under their thick white load, and the little haystacks and avalanche-breaks had completely disappeared. Screwing up their eyes in their wrinkled brown faces, they stared upwards. They shook their heads anxiously, looking more worried every hour. It was too mild for the time of year and the wind was changeable. Just like the year of disaster, 1927.

'Bad, very bad,' muttered John, the bent old road-mender. He had spent the whole day clearing a narrow path along what had been the village street, where the snow now lay in deep drifts between the houses.

'Hi! Look out!' shouted Bartel, the son of Gurtnelli the café owner. Bartel stood on the roof of the café up to his waist in snow, trying again, as he had every day, to shovel down some of the enormously heavy load of snow. But it was a hopeless task. The other villagers had given it up. At night they lay restlessly awake, thinking they heard the roof beams crack under the weight.

'I should call it a day if I were you!' Bartel shouted down to Old John. 'We'd better climb in through the first floor windows. It's much easier than grubbing passages to our front doors.'

But Old John only scowled and went on working away with his broad snow shovel.

'A man must work or else he starts thinking too much,' he grunted.

From time to time there came the heavy thump of the great lumps of snow as Bartel shovelled them off the roof of the café.

'The school kids are having a fine time! They haven't been to school for two days. I never had that when *I* was a kid!' shouted Bartel again. Up there on the roof his young voice would ordinarily have rung out clearly, but now with the thick heavy blanket of snow covering everything and dimming all sounds, his words came dully through the snowflakes that still fluttered slowly down.

'Children are children,' grunted Old John. 'They don't know what's in store for them.'

But Bartel did not hear him. 'I do believe the sun's going to come out,' he shouted. He pointed with outstretched arm to a pale, watery spot in the grey snow cloud.

'We must thank God if it stops snowing,' muttered Old John, looking up.

'Did you say something?' called Bartel, shovelling down another huge block of snow.

But the old road-mender shook his head on its wry neck. 'You youngsters think you know everything,' he called up hoarsely. 'But the Kühelihorn and the Glarbeckscher* will teach you something yet!'

'What?' laughed Bartel looking at the two eastern peaks. He could see them both from where he stood. 'They look quite good and quiet.'

'Oh, yes. Good and quiet. That's what you say,' grumbled Old John. He pulled out his large brown handkerchief to blow his nose. This he did at length and with great thoroughness. When he had finished he called: 'I'm going to find my old woman. She'll have the soup hot for my dinner by now, I expect.' And he trudged off with the broad snow shovel over his shoulder. Round a bend in the path he vanished between the high snow walls which reached to the wooden balconies of the upper storeys.

The villagers had managed to dig little passages running close round the houses from their front doors. A dim twilight showed through the panes of the ground floor windows, except where the heavy wooden shutters were closed and the attempt to clear the snow had been given up. In the little grocer's shop women with aprons over their black coats and shopping baskets on their arms stood gossiping in the feeble light of an unshaded electric bulb. Their faces under their woollen scarves were pale and serious.

'The baker's only got yeast enough to last for three days,' said one.

'Did you hear what the wireless said half an hour ago?' asked another.

Old John did not find his wife at home when he stepped into the dark kitchen. But the saucepan of soup stood on the oil stove. He took off the lid and sniffed.

'Lentil soup,' he murmured, 'but where are the onions?' He shook his head. Of course there were no onions left in the village. All supplies were cut off.

snow covered mountains

From *Avalanche!* by A Rutgers van der Loeff

Title: **Avalanche!**

Author: **A Rutgers van der Loeff**

Narrative perspective: _____

_____

_____

_____

The weather conditions make it possible that an avalanche may occur. The characters have different points of view regarding the weather.

Find clues in the story to show how the author lets the reader know Bartel's point of view: _____

_____

_____

_____

_____

_____

Find clues in the story to show how the author lets the reader know the point of view of the older villagers: _____

_____

_____

_____

_____

_____

_____

Underground to Canada

The Underground Railroad was the name given to the route by which Negro slaves escaped from the southern states of the United States and found safety in the north and Canada before and during the American Civil War. Often those who helped them on their way were Quakers, members of the religious sect also called the Society of Friends.

'I don't trust no white man,' Liza muttered to herself.

The stars were bright that night and there were only the night sounds of lapping water, croaking frogs, and the hollow, chilling hoot of an owl. They walked near the river.

Julilly locked Liza's arm through hers. She could bear her friend's weight as well as her own. The long night walks were making her legs stronger. But Liza grew thinner and weaker. Lester, especially, was uneasy with her.

'Lester won't slow down for nobody.' Julilly knew this in her heart. 'Lester will fight and protect us from slave catchers, but he won't slow down.'

Julilly listened to the plodding steps of gentle Adam behind her. 'Adam and I will carry her if she gets more sickly,' Julilly reassured herself and walked steadily forward along the path that Lester made for them.

It was still dark when the four of them came at last to a sign printed on a large high board beside the river. Lester read aloud – TENNESSEE.

They stopped beside it. The open road settled far enough into the cranebrakes, so that anyone passing by would never guess they were there. Two men on horseback galloped by, one on either side of the road. The moonlight outlined their figures. One of them was fat and carried a whip; the other one had a gun. The four slaves sat immobile as stunned rabbits until the sound of hoof-beats disappeared. Adam was the first to speak.

'That fat man sure did look like Sims.'

'He could be Sims,' Lester agreed. 'The way he beat his horse and waved his whip made me wonder.'

'We'd best stay right where we are for a long time,' Liza cautioned.

Julilly heard another noise. It was the clatter of wagon wheels. It might be Massa Ross. If the fat man was Sims and he turned around and rode back, he would recognize him! The four of them shared the same thought without speaking it. They moved farther back into the cranebrakes.

The wagon came closer. When it reached the Tennessee sign, it stopped. There was silence. Then, three soft calls of the whippoorwill filled the air. It was their signal; but they had to be certain with the possibility of Sims so near.

Julilly knew at once what she had to do.

'Listen,' she whispered to the others, 'if it's somebody trickin' us from the Riley plantation, they'd right away know Lester and Adam and maybe Liza with her bent-up back. They wouldn't know me. I'm just a big, tall nigger boy the way I'm dressed now. I'll go first.'

Lester hesitated, then nodded his approval.

Julilly took a deep breath like she was going to jump into the Mississippi River, and walked into the open.

She stood at the edge of the road and spoke hoarsely.

'Who is you?' Her voice quivered. She couldn't risk revealing the password.

'Friends with a friend,' the man on the wagon answered. It wasn't Massa Ross, but this man knew the right password. Liza, Lester, and Adam came from the shadows. The man relaxed the reins and leaned over the side to see them better. He was brisk and small. It was hard to see his head because a wide-brimmed hat covered most of it. His lips smiled kindly above a white looped-over collar.

'You are friends of Mr Ross,' he said simply. 'The good man has been put in prison in Columbus, Mississippi, and we pray no harm will come to him. I've been sent in his place.'

'Oh, Lord, help him,' Liza prayed aloud.

'Massa,' Lester interrupted, 'two slave-hunters just passed by this way goin' north. We think they are from our place – the Riley plantation.'

'Then we must hide you at once and talk later.' The little man jumped to the ground. He threw back a large canvas that covered the wagon. Underneath was a thick layer of fresh straw.

'You must crawl under the straw towards the centre.' He spoke swiftly like someone familiar with his task. 'Then I will cover you with the canvas. If we are stopped, remain silent. I will do the talking.'

From *Underground to Canada* by Barbara Smucker

Character's name: _____

What the character says and does:

- when he or she is walking along _____

_____

_____

_____

_____

_____

- when he or she is hiding in the cranebrakes _____

_____

_____

_____

_____

_____

- when he or she steps out onto the road _____

_____

_____

_____

_____

_____

- when he or she is speaking with the wagon driver _____

_____

_____

_____

_____

_____

Performance poetry

Learning targets

On completion of this unit the children should be able to:

1 ➤➤ read, rehearse and modify performance of poetry
2 ➤➤ select poetry, justify their choices, e.g. in compiling class anthology

Before you start

Background knowledge

The examples of performance poetry in this unit (**Copymasters 32** and **33**) are from *Poetry Jump-Up* compiled by Grace Nichols. Performance poetry is poetry which lends itself to group performance and has opportunities for different voices within the group to perform different parts of the poem. Narrative poems with dialogue are particularly suitable for this work.

Resources for Session 1

Copymaster 32 Old Men of Magic
Copymaster 33 On aging

Resources for Session 2

A selection of poetry anthologies from a variety of traditions and cultures.
Copymaster 34 Choosing a poem

Assessment indicators

- Can the children work as a group to choose, practise and perform an appropriate poem?

Teaching the sessions

Session 1 ①

Introduction [20-25 min]

▨ Explain to the children that in this session you are going to be looking at ways in which poetry can be performed by a group in interesting ways.

Give each child **Copymaster 32 Old Men of Magic** and read it to the class while they follow. Discuss the impact of the poem with the children.

- What is it about?
- Who are the 'old men of magic'?
- What visual images does it conjure up for them?

If time allows, let the children do a quick sketch to show their interpretation of the scene the poem depicts. Ensure they have grasped that it is night in the poem.

Performing a poem [20-30 min]

⬧ Put the children into small groups and explain that they are going to prepare this poem to read to the rest of the class. Give them time for group discussion as to how they might do this and then go round to each group, listening to their suggestions. Discourage them from just reading the whole poem as a group. Ask:

- how can the poem be divided between different voices?
- in what tone will different parts of the poem be read?
- if there is a climax in the poem which the speed and volume of the performance can work up to? For example:
  First 7 lines: a whole group, fairly 'ordinary' reading
  Next 10 lines: build-up of speed and volume, individual voices for each line, then long pause
  Last 4 lines: whole group conclusion

Give each group as much space as possible out of the hearing of the other groups to practise and polish their performance.

Summary [15-20 min]

▨ Each group should perform the poem for the rest of the class. After each group, discuss the way the poem was performed. Let the 'audience' question the group as to why certain lines were delivered as they were, e.g. the speed, volume, individual voice, etc. Make this as constructive an experience for the children as possible.

On aging   `20-30min`

Give each group **Copymaster 33 On Aging** (explain that the poem contains the American spelling of 'ageing') and instruct them to read the poem and discuss what it is about. What is the poet's attitude to being old? How does she want to be treated?

Listen to the group discussions and when you feel a group has understood the poem, let them begin to prepare it for performance. Time should be made available for each group to perform the poem for the class.

Session 2   ②

Introduction   `15min`

Explain to the children that they are going to look through poetry anthologies for poems which they think would be suitable for performance. Look at examples of poems with repeated lines or choruses and discuss how these would be handled in a group performance. Ask the children what sort of poetry they think would be suitable; some may be able to give you specific examples.

Choosing a poem   `20-30min`

The children should work in small groups and use **Copymaster 33 Choosing a poem** to record their discussion.

Summary   `10-15 min`

Each group should appoint a spokesperson to report back to the class about the group's choice of poem, giving the reasons for their choice.

The poems should be copied and compiled as a class anthology.

Each group should be given time to practise, polish and perform their poem for the class.

Old Men of Magic

Old men of magic
with beards long and aged,
speak tales on evenings,
tales so entrancing,
we sit and we listen,
to whispery secrets
about the earth and the heavens.
And late at night,
after sundown they speak
of spirits that live
in silk cotton trees,
of frightening shadows
that sneak through the dark,
and bright balls of fire
that fly in night air,
of shapes unimaginable,
we gasp and we gape,
then just as we're scared
old men of magic
wave hands rough and wrinkled
and all trace of fear disappears

Dionne Brand

On Aging

When you see me sitting quietly,
Like a sack left on the shelf,
Don't think I need your chattering.
I'm listening to myself.
Hold! Stop! Don't pity me!
Hold! Stop your sympathy!
Understanding if you got it,
Otherwise I'll do without it!

When my bones are stiff and aching
And my feet won't climb the stair,
I will only ask one favour:
Don't bring me no rocking chair.

When you see me walking, stumbling,
Don't study and get it wrong.
'Cause tired don't mean lazy
And every goodbye ain't gone.
I'm the same person I was back then,
A little less hair, a little less chin,
A lot less lungs and much less wind.
But ain't I lucky I can still breathe in.

Maya Angelou

34 | Choosing a poem

Poetry books we looked at:

Titles and authors of poems we considered:

The poem we chose is: _____

We chose it to perform because: _____

_____

_____

_____

UNIT 3 | Older literature

Learning targets

On completion of this unit the children should be able to:

►► explore the challenge and appeal of older literature through:
- listening to older literature being read aloud
- reading accessible poems, stories and extracts
- reading extracts from classic serials shown on television
- discussing differences in language used

►► write in the style of the author, e.g. writing on to complete a section, resolve a conflict; writing additional dialogue, new chapter.

Before you start

Background knowledge

This is a set of ambitious objectives given the linguistic difficulty of the material and the amount that should be read to realistically 'explore the challenge and appeal'.

The practical way forward is to choose an author or theme and look at extracts set against some initial research into the period in question. This unit deals with poor children in the Victorian age at school and work.

Resources for Session 1

Copymaster 35 Victorian children
Books, magazine articles, CD-ROMs, etc. for the children to use to research what life was like for children in the Victorian age.

Resources for Session 2

Copymaster 36 Oliver asks for more!
Copymaster 37 Jane Eyre

Resources for Session 3

Copymaster 38 Oliver's first job
Copymaster 39 The Water-babies

Assessment indicators

- Can the children explain why they do, or do not, like the extracts?
- Can they identify the language and style of older literature?

Teaching the sessions

Session 1 ①

Introduction [10-30 min]

▦ Begin by ascertaining what the children already know about what children's lives were like in the nineteenth century. The class may have studied the Victorians or they may have seen classic serials on television, giving them an insight into what life was like over one hundred years ago.

Copymaster 35 Victorian children gives some basic facts about the lives of both well-off and poor children. This can be used as a whole class text for discussion, or the children can work on it in groups.

Victorian children [20 min]

◆◆ Each group should read and discuss **Copymaster 35**, focusing on any facts they find surprising, e.g.

compulsory education only until the age of 10; and their opinions, e.g. do they think the lives of children were better or worse in Victorian times?

Summary [10-15 min]

▦ Discuss the children's reaction to what they have read. How do they feel about parents who sent their children out to work such long hours? Can they see the economic necessity for this? Through discussion, build up a picture of how different life was for most children to give the class a factual background against which the extracts in the following session can be read.

Research [20-30 min]

▮ Using resources from the classroom, school library and home, ask the children to read about the Victorian age and make notes on three or more facts which relate to the lives of children. Remind them of the usefulness of the contents page and index, and of the key word approach to making notes.

If time allows, discuss what the children have discovered. The facts should be kept to form part of a class display which will feature their own writing from Sessions 2 and 3. They can be written neatly or word processed to provide a factual element to the display.

Session 2

Introduction `10-30min`

🏁 This session concentrates on two extracts which illustrate the hardships faced by Victorian children.

Copymaster 36 Oliver asks for more! is the classic scene from *Oliver Twist* where, driven by hunger, the boys in the workhouse decide that one of their number should ask for a second helping of gruel.

Copymaster 37 Jane Eyre tells of an incident early in Jane's stay at Lowood School where another girl is severely punished without good reason.

These copymasters can be used for whole class or group discussion.

If they are to be used in groups, several groups can have one copymaster and several the other, and report to the class on the conditions experienced by the children in the extract. They should be instructed to:

• outline the plot of the extract, i.e. what happens

• highlight the difference (or similarities!) to present day schooling

• express the group's opinion of the treatment of the children in the extract.

The language is difficult and you should be on hand to aid each group's discussion where vocabulary hinders their understanding of the text.

When each group has delivered their findings, spend some time on discussing the language. Did the children find it difficult? Can they find examples of words and phrases which are not commonly used today?

Writing on ... `30min`

👤 Explain to the children that they are going to 'write on' from the extract they have read. Either:

• continue the story of Oliver after he has asked for more gruel. The final sentences give a clue as to how his request has been received. What will the master do? How will Oliver be punished?

Or

• write a conversation between Jane and Helen after the latter has been beaten by Miss Scatcherd. Jane is angry on her friend's behalf and there are clues in the text as to how Helen has taken her punishment. What does Jane think Helen should do? Why did Helen not protest that she had done nothing wrong?

Encourage the children to work in draft form and discuss their work with you before making a neat copy. The children's work, along with the facts they researched in Session 1, can form a display on 'Children in Victorian Times'.

Session 3

Introduction `10-30min`

🏁 This session concentrates on two extracts showing the working lives of poor boys in the Victorian age.

Copymaster 38 Oliver's first job is an account of his first evening with his employers, Mr and Mrs Sowerberry, the undertakers.

Copymaster 39 The Water-babies is the opening of the story which introduces the young chimney-sweep, Tom, and the beginning of his adventures.

These copymasters can be used for whole class or group discussion.

If they are to be used in groups, several groups can have one copymaster and several the other, and report to the class on the working conditions described in the extract. They should be instructed to:

• outline the plot of the extract, i.e. what happens

• highlight the difference from present day employment of children

• express the group's opinion of the treatment of the children in the extract.

The language is difficult and you should be on hand to aid each group's discussion where vocabulary hinders their understanding of the text.

When each group has delivered their findings, spend some time discussing the language. Did the children find it difficult? Can they find examples of words and phrases which are not commonly used today?

Writing on ... `30min`

👤 Explain to the children that they are going to 'write on' from the extract they have read. Either:

• think carefully about the situation Oliver finds himself in with no choice but to work for the Sowerberrys, being fed on the dog's scraps and having to sleep under the counter among the coffins. Imagine you are Oliver and write about your thoughts and feelings on that first night in the eerie darkness. What are you going to do?

Or

• What happens in the room that Tom has mistakenly arrived in? Why is it a room 'the like of which he had never seen before'? Is there anyone else in the room? What do they talk about? Continue the story.

Encourage the children to work in draft form and discuss their work with you before making a neat copy. The children's work can be added to the display on 'Children in Victorian Times'.

Victorian children

At school

A variety of schools existed throughout the nineteenth century. Wealthier parents were able to send their children to fee-paying grammar, public and private schools. Poor children had schools provided either by the Church of England (National Schools), the Roman Catholic Church or by the Nonconformist churches (British and Foreign Schools). Dame schools, workhouse schools, charity schools and ragged schools also existed for poor children. Older pupils, called monitors, often assisted teachers in these schools.

Four important dates in the development of Victorian education are:

1862 *The Revised Code of Education* introduced a 'payment by results' scheme. A grant was made to a school only if attendance and the standard of its pupils' work met the requirements of inspectors.

1870 *The Forster Education Act* made provision for new schools to be built in areas where there were insufficient voluntary ones. These schools soon became known as Board Schools after the local school boards that were set up with responsibility for their building.

1880 Education was made compulsory up to the age of ten. Absenteeism remained high in some areas where parents, out of economic necessity, still sent their children to work.

1891 Elementary education was made free.

Victorian children (cont.)

At home

Free time, leisure and hobbies were unknown to poorer children. Middle and upper-class Victorian children were supposed to occupy themselves with quiet and worthwhile pursuits without distracting adults. Collecting and arranging natural history exhibits, compiling scrapbooks, making gifts and playing a variety of board and card games were all very popular.

At work

For most of the first half of the nineteenth century, child labour was an accepted way of Victorian life. Laws were passed to try to improve conditions and by 1847 no child between the ages of 13 and 18 was to work in a factory for more than ten hours a day!

Oliver asks for more!

Oliver Twist was born in the workhouse and left an orphan to be educated and found employment by the boards which ran the workhouse. These places were grim and forbidding and life was very hard for the people who were so poor that they had no choice but to live there. They worked long hours and the food was meagre.

In this extract, Oliver has been chosen to ask for a second helping of gruel at supper time.

The room in which the boys were fed was a large stone hall, with a copper at one end; out of which the master, dressed in an apron for the purpose, and assisted by one or two women, ladled the gruel at meal-times. Of this festive composition each boy had one porringer, and no more – except on occasions of great public rejoicing, when he had two ounces and a quarter of bread besides. The bowls never wanted washing. The boys polished them with their spoons till they shone again; and when they had performed this operation (which never took very long, the spoons being nearly as large as the bowls), they would sit staring at the copper, with such eager eyes, as if they could have devoured the very bricks of which it was composed; employing themselves, meanwhile, in sucking their fingers most assiduously, with the view of catching up any stray splashes of gruel that might have been cast thereon. Boys have generally excellent appetites. Oliver Twist and his companions suffered the tortures of slow starvation for three months. At last they got so voracious and wild with hunger, that one boy who was tall for his age, and hadn't been used to that sort of thing (for his father had kept a small cook's shop), hinted darkly to his companions, that unless he had another basin of gruel per diem, he was afraid he might some night happen to eat the boy who slept next him, who happened to be a weakly youth of tender age. He had a wild, hungry eye; and they implicitly believed him. A council was held; lots were cast who should walk up to the master after supper that evening and ask for more; and it fell to Oliver Twist.

The evening arrived, the boys took their places. The master, in his cook's uniform, stationed himself at the copper; his pauper assistants ranged themselves behind him; the gruel was served out; and a long grace was said over the short commons. The gruel disappeared; the boys whispered to each other, and winked at Oliver; while his next neighbours nudged him. Child as he was, he was desperate with hunger, and reckless with misery. He rose from the table; and advancing to the master, basin and spoon in hand, said, somewhat alarmed at his own temerity, –

'Please, sir, I want some more.'

The master was a fat, healthy man; but he turned very pale. He gazed in stupefied astonishment on the small rebel for some seconds; and then clung for support to the copper. The assistants were paralysed with wonder, the boys with fear.

From *Oliver Twist* by Charles Dickens

Jane Eyre

Jane Eyre, an orphan, has been sent to Lowood School. On the first day she makes the acquaintance of Helen Burns on the veranda. This extract is Jane's second day at Lowood.

At first, being little accustomed to learn by heart, the lessons appeared to me both long and difficult: the frequent change from task to task, too, bewildered me; and I was glad, when, about three o'clock in the afternoon, Miss Smith put into my hands a border of muslin two yards long, together with needle, thimble, etc., and sent me to sit in a quiet corner of the schoolroom, with directions to hem the same. At that hour most of the others were sewing likewise; but one class still stood round Miss Scatcherd's chair reading, and as all was quiet, the subject of their lessons could be heard, together with the manner in which each girl acquitted herself, and the animadversions or commendations of Miss Scatcherd on the performance. It was English history: among the readers, I observed my acquaintance of the veranda; at the commencement of the lesson, her place had been at the top of the class, but for some error of pronunciation or some inattention to stops, she was suddenly sent to the very bottom. Even in that obscure position, Miss Scatcherd continued to make her an object of constant notice; she was continually addressing to her such phrases as the following: –

'Burns (such it seems was her name: the girls here were all called by their surnames, as boys are elsewhere), Burns, you are standing on the side of your shoe, turn your toes out immediately.' 'Burns, you poke your chin most unpleasantly; draw it in.' 'Burns, I insist on your holding your head up; I will not have you before me in that attitude,' etc., etc.

A chapter having been read through twice, the books were closed and the girls examined. The lesson had comprised part of the reign of Charles I, and there were sundry questions about tonnage, and poundage, and ship-money, which most of them appeared unable to answer; still every little difficulty was solved instantly when it reached Burns: her memory seemed to have retained the substance of the whole lesson, and she was ready with answers on every point. I kept expecting that Miss Scatcherd would praise her attention; but, instead of that, she suddenly cried out –

'You dirty, disagreeable girl! you have never cleaned your nails this morning!'

Burns made no answer: I wondered at her silence.

'Why,' thought I, 'does she not explain that she could neither clean her nails nor wash her face, as the water was frozen?'

My attention was now called off by Miss Smith desiring me to hold a skein of thread: while she was winding it, she talked to me from time to time, asking whether I had ever been at school before, whether I could mark, stitch, knit etc.; till she dismissed me, I could not pursue my observations on Miss Scatcherd's movements. When I returned to my seat, that lady was just delivering an order, of which I did not catch the import; but Burns immediately left the class, and going into the small inner room where the books were kept, returned in half a minute, carrying in her hand a bundle of twigs tied together at one end. This ominous tool she presented to Miss Scatcherd with a respectful curtsey; then she quietly and without being told, unloosed her pinafore, and the teacher instantly and sharply inflicted on her neck a dozen strokes with the bunch of twigs. Not a tear rose to Burn's eye; and, while I paused from my sewing, because my fingers quivered at this spectacle with a sentiment of unavailing and impotent anger, not a feature of her pensive face altered its ordinary expression.

'Hardened girl!' exclaimed Miss Scatcherd; 'nothing can correct you of your slatternly habits: carry the rod away.'

Burns obeyed: I looked at her narrowly as she emerged from the book closet; she was just putting back her handkerchief into her pocket, and the trace of a tear glistened on her thin cheek.

From *Jane Eyre* by Charlotte Brontë

Oliver's first job

Oliver, after daring to ask for more gruel, is punished by being locked in a dark room. The adults who run the workhouse decide that Oliver must be sold to someone who is willing to give him work. He finds himself taken by Mr Bumble to Mr Sowerberry, a local undertaker.

The undertaker, who had just put up the shutters of his shop, was making some entries in his day-book by the light of a most appropriately dismal candle, when Mr Bumble entered.

'Aha!' said the undertaker, looking up from the book, and pausing in the middle of a word; 'is that you, Bumble?'

'No one else, Mr Sowerberry,' replied the beadle. 'Here, I've brought the boy.' Oliver made a bow.

'Oh! that's the boy, is it?' said the undertaker, raising the candle above his head, to get a better view of Oliver. 'Mrs Sowerberry! will you have the goodness to come here a moment, my dear?'

Mrs Sowerberry emerged from a little room behind the shop, and presented the form of a short, thin, squeezed-up woman, with a vixenish countenance.

'My dear,' said Mr Sowerberry, deferentially, 'this is the boy from the workhouse that I told you of.' Oliver bowed again.

'Dear me!' said the undertaker's wife, 'he's very small.'

'Why, he *is* rather small,' replied Mr Bumble, looking at Oliver as if it were his fault that he was no bigger; 'he *is* small. There's no denying it. But he'll grow, Mrs Sowerberry – he'll grow.'

'Ah! I dare say he will,' replied the lady pettishly, 'on our victuals and our drink. I see no saving in parish children, not I; for they always cost more to keep than they're worth. However, men always think they know best. There! Get downstairs, little bag o'bones.' With this the undertaker's wife opened a side door, and pushed Oliver down a steep flight of stairs into a stone cell, damp and dark, forming the ante-room to the coal-cellar, and denominated 'the kitchen': wherein sat a slatternly girl, in shoes down at heel, and blue worsted stockings very much out of repair.

'Here, Charlotte,' said Mrs Sowerberry, who had followed Oliver down, 'give this boy some of the cold bits that were put by for Trip. He hasn't come home since the morning, so he may go without 'em. I daresay the boy isn't too dainty to eat 'em – are you boy?'

Oliver's first job (cont.)

Oliver, whose eyes had glistened at the mention of meat, and who was trembling with eagerness to devour it, replied in the negative; and a plateful of coarse broken victuals was set before him …

'Well,' said the undertaker's wife, when Oliver had finished his supper … 'have you done?'

There being nothing eatable within his reach, Oliver replied in the affirmative.

'Then come with me,' said Mrs Sowerberry, taking up a dim and dirty lamp, and leading the way upstairs; 'your bed's under the counter. You don't mind sleeping among the coffins, I suppose? But it doesn't much matter whether you do or don't, for you can't sleep anywhere else. Come – don't keep me here all night!'

Oliver lingered no longer, but meekly followed his new mistress.

From *Oliver Twist* by Charles Dickens

The Water-babies

At the beginning of the story we are introduced to Tom, a young boy who earns a few pence by crawling through the chimneys of large houses and cleaning them.

Once upon a time there was a little chimney-sweep, and his name was Tom. That is a short name, and you have heard it before, so you will not have much trouble in remembering it. He lived in a great town in the North country, where there were plenty of chimneys to sweep, and plenty of money for Tom to earn and his master to spend. He could not read nor write, and did not care to do either; and he never washed himself, for there was no water up the court where he lived. He had never been taught to say his prayers. He never had heard of God, or of Christ, except in words which you never have heard, and which it would have been well if he had never heard. He cried half his time, and laughed the other half. He cried when he had to climb the dark flues, rubbing his poor knees and elbows raw; and when the soot got into his eyes, which it did every day in the week; and when his master beat him, which he did every day in the week; and when he had not enough to eat, which happened every day in the week likewise. And he laughed the other half of the day, when he was tossing halfpennies with the other boys, or playing leap-frog over the posts, or bowling stones at the horses' legs as they trotted by, which last was excellent fun, when there was a wall at hand behind which to hide. As for chimney-sweeping, and being hungry, and being beaten, he took all that for the way of the world …

The Water-babies (cont.)

One chimney-sweeping job that Tom has to do is at Harthover House, a grand place with lots of chimneys! He arrives with his master, Grimes, at the iron gates to the house.

But Tom and his master did not go in through the great iron gates, as if they had been Dukes or Bishops, but round the back way, and a very long way round it was; and into a little back door, where the ash-boy let them in, yawning horribly; and then in a passage the housekeeper met them, in such a flowered chintz dressing-gown, that Tom mistook her for my lady herself, and she gave Grimes solemn orders about 'You will take care of this, and take care of that,' as if he was going up the chimneys, and not Tom. And Grimes listened, and said every now and then, under his voice, 'You'll mind that, you little beggar?' and Tom did mind, all at least that he could. And then the housekeeper turned them into a grand room, all covered up in sheets of brown paper, and bade them begin, in a lofty and tremendous voice; and so after a whimper or two, and a kick from his master, into the grate Tom went, and up the chimney, while a housemaid stayed in the room to watch the furniture …

How many chimneys he swept I cannot say: but he swept so many that he got quite tired, and puzzled, too, for they were not like the town flues to which he was accustomed, but such as you would find – if you would only get up them and look, which perhaps you would not like to do – in old country houses, large and crooked chimneys, which had been altered again and again … So Tom fairly lost his way in them; not that he cared much for that, though he was in pitchy darkness, for he was as much at home in a chimney as a mole is underground; but at last, coming down as he thought the right chimney he came down the wrong one, and found himself standing on the hearthrug in a room the like of which he had never seen before.

From *The Water-babies* by Charles Kingsley

40

Points of view

Look carefully at the picture.
The two girls will have different points of view on what is happening.

The girl doing the tripping up	**The girl being tripped up**
Why is she doing this?	Is she surprised?
Is she paying the other girl back in some way?	Would she expect the other girl to do this?
What is she thinking?	Has she offended the other girl in some way?
What is her attitude to the other girl?	How does she feel about what is happening?

Imagine that what is happening in the picture is an incident in a story which each girl later recounts to her friends.

Write about the incident from both viewpoints. Make sure your reader knows the thoughts and feelings of each girl and how their view on the incident differs.

YEAR 6 TERM 1

Focus

In this section the children will be given the opportunity to:

1 investigate literature by long-established authors
2 read an extract from a Shakespeare play and produce a modern retelling
3 produce a playscript from a story extract.

Content

Unit 1: Shakespeare
Unit 2: Playscripts

Extract list

Aiken, Joan: *The Wolves of Willoughby Chase*
Juster, Norton: *The Phantom Tollbooth*
Nesbit, E.: *The Railway Children*
Shakespeare, William: *Hamlet*

Assessment

Assessment Copymaster 51 is at the end of the section.

Copymaster 51 Writing a playscript gives the children the opportunity to use an extract of their choice and draw on their knowledge of staging conventions to produce a playscript.

This chart shows you how to find activities by unit to resource your term's requirements for text level work on fiction. The Learning Targets closely follow the structure of the fiction requirements for the term in the National Literacy Strategy document (pages 50–51). A few of the requirements are not covered.

YEAR 6 Term 1

Range

Fiction:

- classic fiction and drama by long-established authors including, where appropriate, study of a Shakespeare play

TEXT LEVEL WORK

COMPREHENSION AND COMPOSITION

Reading comprehension

Pupils should be taught:

3 to articulate personal responses to literature, identifying why and how a text affects the reader; Unit 1

4 to be familiar with the work of some established authors, to know what is special about their work; Unit 1

5 to contribute constructively to shared discussion about literature, responding to and building on the views of others; Unit 1

Writing composition

Pupils should be taught:

6 to produce a modern retelling; Unit 1

9 to prepare a short section of story as a script, e.g. using stage directions, location/setting; Unit 2

UNIT 1 | Shakespeare

Learning targets

On completion of this unit the children should be able to:

1 ➡➤ articulate personal responses to literature, identifying why and how a text affects the reader

2 ➡➤ be familiar with the work of some established authors, to know what is special about their work

3 ➡➤ contribute constructively to shared discussion about literature, responding to and building on the views of others

4 ➡➤ produce a modern retelling.

Before you start

Background knowledge

This unit concentrates on introducing the children to an extract of Shakespearean text from *Hamlet*. The appearance of Hamlet's father's ghost is a very powerful piece and should illicit a variety of responses from the children.

You may decide to read a story version of Hamlet, for example from Ian Serraillier's *The Enchanted Island*, before the children embark on this unit, or to finish off the work by letting them know how the story unfolds and ends.

Resources for Session 1

Collected Works of Shakespeare
Copymaster 41 The story so far …
Copymaster 42 The Ghost appears
Copymaster 43 The Ghost appears, annotated version
Copymaster 44 Setting the scene

Resources for Session 2

Copymaster 45 The Ghost speaks
Copymaster 46 The Ghost speaks, annotated version

Links to other units

Learning Targets: Non-Fiction Years 5 and 6 Year 6 Term 1 Unit 1 – Biography and autobiography (William Shakespeare)

Assessment indicators

- Can the children read a demanding extract and contribute to a discussion on a literal basis?
- Can they produce a modern retelling of a long-established author?

Teaching the sessions

Session 1 ① ② ③

Introduction [30 min]

▨ Begin by ascertaining what the children already know about Shakespeare. Copymaster 34 from *Learning Targets: Non-Fiction Years 5 and 6* can be read to the children to give them some background information on Shakespeare (see Links to other units). Alternatively you could set a research task for the children and pool the information about Shakespeare in a class discussion.

Can the children name any of Shakespeare's plays?

Have they ever been to see one?

Show the children the collected works of Shakespeare to give them some idea of how prolific a writer he was. Explain that the plays fall into three main categories:

- comedies
- histories
- tragedies.

Discuss these categories to ensure the children understand them in broad terms.

The extract you are going to look at is from one of Shakespeare's greatest tragedies, *Hamlet*.

Give each child **Copymaster 41 The story so far …** and read it through with them. Can they make any predictions as to why the ghost of Hamlet's father is appearing on the battlements?

Explain to the children that you are now going to look at the scene where Hamlet is waiting with Horatio and Marcellus and the Ghost appears again. Give each child **Copymaster 42 The Ghost appears**. At this stage it is advisable that you read the scene as the children follow.

Ask for immediate responses. These may range from a lack of understanding, to comments on the difficulty of the language, to 'that was scary!'. Spend some time analysing the text with the children so that the language does not remain a barrier to their understanding of what is going on. **Copymaster 43 The Ghost appears, annotated version** will help you if you are unfamiliar with the play. It is at your discretion whether this is photocopied and given to the children.

Discussion

In groups the children should discuss:
- what they think Hamlet wants the ghost to tell him
- why Marcellus does not want Hamlet to go with the ghost
- why Hamlet is determined to go
- why Marcellus and Horatio decide to follow.

They should also spend some time visualising the scene, i.e.
- how they would set it on stage
- how they would light it
- how they would dress the actors
- how they would present the ghost, e.g. as an unearthly voice, as a real person, etc.
- how they would want the audience to feel.

Summary 15-20min

Investigate the groups' findings through class discussion.

Setting the scene 20-25min

Copymaster 44 Setting the scene gives the children an outline of a traditional, curtained (proscenium arch) stage on which they are to draw and colour the set and position the actors. Space is given at the bottom for notes to explain the intended audience reaction by setting the scene in this way.

Session 2

Introduction 30min

Follow the format of Session 1 using **Copymaster 45 The Ghost speaks** and **Copymaster 46 The Ghost speaks, annotated version**. This scene is the meeting between Hamlet and his ghostly father.

Discussion 20-30min

The children should discuss:
- why the ghost has appeared to Hamlet
- what the Ghost wants Hamlet to do
- how the people of Denmark think he died
- how he actually died.

They should also spend some time on visualising the scene, i.e.
- how they would set it on stage
- how they would light it
- how they would want the audience to feel.

Summary 15-20min

Investigate the groups' findings through class discussion.

Session 3

Preparing a modern retelling 30+ min

The first activity in this session should be group based. Groups of four can script the first scene from **Copymaster 42** in modern English and prepare the scripts for performance.

Each member of the group can take the part of one of the characters: Hamlet, Marcellus, Horatio and the Ghost.

They should:
- draw their character in costume and annotate the drawing to show exactly how that character appears
- make notes on how that character would feel at various points in the scene
- make notes on how they want the audience to feel about that character
- contribute to a modern translation of the lines in the scene.

Scene 2 30+ min

Each child can script the scene from **Copymaster 45** in modern English.

41

The story so far ...

Hamlet, the young Prince of Denmark, returns from University to find that his father, King Hamlet, is dead. His mother, Queen Gertrude, has quickly married Claudius, her dead husband's brother and Hamlet's uncle.

Hamlet is very upset by the death of his father and how speedily his mother has remarried. Gertrude is upset because Hamlet will not join in the wedding celebrations. He has a feeling that all is not right and he does not trust his uncle, Claudius.

Some of Hamlet's friends come to tell him of a strange happening which occurred when they were on watch late at night. A spirit, dressed in armour and looking exactly like the dead king, has appeared to them. Hamlet wants to know what the ghost has said but, although they tried to speak to it, the ghost did not reply.

Hamlet makes up his mind to watch for the ghost that very night. He arranges to meet the others on the battlements between eleven and midnight.

The Ghost appears

Hamlet, Horatio and Marcellus are on the battlements just before midnight. They have been talking in quiet voices about the party which Claudius is having in the castle.

Enter GHOST

HORATIO: Look, my lord, it comes.

HAMLET: Angels and ministers of grace defend us!
Be thou a spirit of health or goblin damn'd,
Bring with thee airs from heaven or blasts from hell,
Be thy intents wicked or charitable,
Thou com'st in such a questionable shape
That I will speak to thee. I'll call thee Hamlet,
King, father, royal Dane. O answer me.
Let me not burst in ignorance, but tell
Why thy canoniz'd bones, hearsed in death,
Have burst their cerements, why the sepulchre
Wherein we saw thee quietly inurn'd
Hath op'd his ponderous and marble jaws
To cast thee up again. What may this mean,
That thou, dead corse, again in complete steel
Revisits thus the glimpses of the moon,
Making night hideous and we fools of nature
So horridly to shake our disposition
With thoughts beyond the reaches of our souls?
Say why is this? Wherefore? What should we do?

GHOST *beckons.*

HORATIO: It beckons you to go away with it,
As if it some impartment did desire
To you alone.

MARCELLUS: Look with what courteous action
It waves you to a more removed ground.
But do not go with it.

HORATIO: No, by no means.

HAMLET: It will not speak. Then I will follow it.

HORATIO: Do not, my lord.

HAMLET: Why, what should be the fear?
I do not set my life at a pin's fee,
And for my soul, what can it do to that,
Being a thing immortal as itself?
It waves me forth again. I'll follow it.

HORATIO: What if it tempt you toward the flood, my lord,
Or to the dreadful summit of the cliff
That beetles o'er his base into the sea,
And there assume some other horrible form
Which might deprive your sovereignty of reason
And draw you into madness? Think of it.
The very place puts toys of desperation,
Without more motive, into every brain
That looks so many fathoms to the sea
And hears it roar beneath.

HAMLET: It waves me still.
Go on, I'll follow thee.

MARCELLUS: You shall not go, my lord.

HAMLET: Hold off your hands.

HORATIO: Be rul'd; you shall not go.

HAMLET: My fate cries out
And makes each petty artire in this body
As hardy as the Nemean lion's nerve.
Still am I call'd. Unhand me, gentlemen.
By heaven, I'll make a ghost of him that lets me.
I say away. – Go on, I'll follow thee.

                                    Exeunt GHOST *and* HAMLET.

HORATIO: He waxes desperate with imagination.

MARCELLUS: Let's follow. 'Tis not fit thus to obey him.

HORATIO: Have after. To what issue will this come?

MARCELLUS: Something is rotten in the state of Denmark.

HORATIO: Heaven will direct it.

MARCELLUS: Nay, let's follow him.

                                                        Exeunt.
                                    From *Hamlet* by William Shakespeare

The Ghost appears, annotated version

Hamlet, Horatio and Marcellus are on the battlements just before midnight. They have been talking in quiet voices about the party which Claudius is having in the castle.

Enter GHOST

HORATIO: Look, my lord, it comes.

HAMLET: **Angels and ministers** of grace defend us!

a prayer for protection against evil spirits

messengers of God

Be thou **a spirit of health** or **goblin damn'd**,

good angel / evil spirit

Bring with thee **airs** from heaven or blasts from hell,

breezes

Be thy **intents** wicked or charitable,

intentions

Hamlet is still not sure but decides to go along with the probability that this is his father's spirit

Thou com'st in such a **questionable** shape

a form which invites questions

That I will speak to thee. I'll call thee Hamlet,

King, father, royal Dane. O answer me.

Let me not burst in ignorance, but tell

Why thy **canoniz'd** bones, **hearsed** in death,

received a Christian burial / put in a coffin

Have burst their **cerements**, why the **sepulchre**

burial clothes / burial tomb

the tomb is seen as an animal with jaws

Wherein we saw thee quietly **inurn'd**

entombed

Hath **op'd** his ponderous and marble jaws

opened

To cast thee up again. What may this mean,

That thou, dead **corse**, again in **complete steel**   *corpse / suit of armour*

Revisits thus the glimpses of the moon,

Making night **hideous** and we **fools** of nature   *terrifying / playthings*

to upset and bewilder us with what we cannot understand ——— So horridly to shake our disposition

With thoughts beyond the reaches of our souls?

Say why is this? Wherefore? What should we do?

GHOST *beckons*.

it wants you to go with it, as if it has something to tell you alone

HORATIO: It beckons you to go away with it,

As if it some impartment did desire

the ghost is not threatening To you alone.

MARCELLUS: Look with what courteous action

Marcellus still believes it could be an evil spirit It waves you to a more removed ground.

Horatio thinks so too But do not go with it.

HORATIO: No, by no means.

Hamlet is determined to find out what the ghost wants HAMLET: It will not speak. Then I will follow it.

HORATIO: Do not, my lord.

HAMLET: Why, what should be the fear?

Hamlet does
not care if ——————⌐ I do not set my life at a pin's fee,
he lives or
dies

And for my soul, what can it do to that,

the ghost
cannot ——————⌐ Being a thing **immortal** as itself?   *not able to*
harm   *be killed*
Hamlet's
soul

It waves me forth again. I'll follow it.

Horatio is   HORATIO: ⌐ What if it tempt you toward the **flood**, my lord,   *sea*
afraid that
the ghost ——————┤ Or to the dreadful summit of the cliff
will get
Hamlet on
his own   That **beetles o'er** his base into the sea,   *overhangs*
and then
turn into
something   And there assume some other horrible form
so hideous,
Hamlet will
be driven   Which might deprive your sovereignty of reason
mad and
kill himself
                 And draw you into madness? Think of it.

                 The very place puts **toys of desperation**,   *irrational*
                                                                                impulses

                 Without more motive, into every brain

                 That looks so many fathoms to the sea

                 And hears it roar beneath.

HAMLET: It waves me still.

Go on, I'll follow thee.

MARCELLUS: You shall not go, my lord.

HAMLET: Hold off your hands.

HORATIO: Be rul'd; you shall not go.

HAMLET: My fate cries out

And makes each petty **artire** in this body   *artery*

As **hardy** as the **Nemean lion's** nerve.   *strong / the mythical lion slai by the Greek her Hercules*

Still am I call'd. Unhand me, gentlemen.

Hamlet threatens to harm anyone who hinders him —— By heaven, I'll make a ghost of him that lets me.

I say away. – Go on, I'll follow thee.

                         Exeunt GHOST *and* HAMLET.   *Hamlet and Ghos leave*

he is behaving like a madman — HORATIO: He waxes desperate with imagination.

MARCELLUS: Let's follow. 'Tis not fit thus to obey him.

HORATIO: **Have after**. To what issue will this come?   *let's pursue him*

MARCELLUS: Something is rotten in the state of Denmark.

God will see to it — HORATIO: Heaven will direct it.

No, let's not leave it to heaven but do something ourselves — MARCELLUS: Nay, let's follow him.

                                        Exeunt.   *Latin – exit of mo than one person*

From *Hamlet* by William Shakespeare

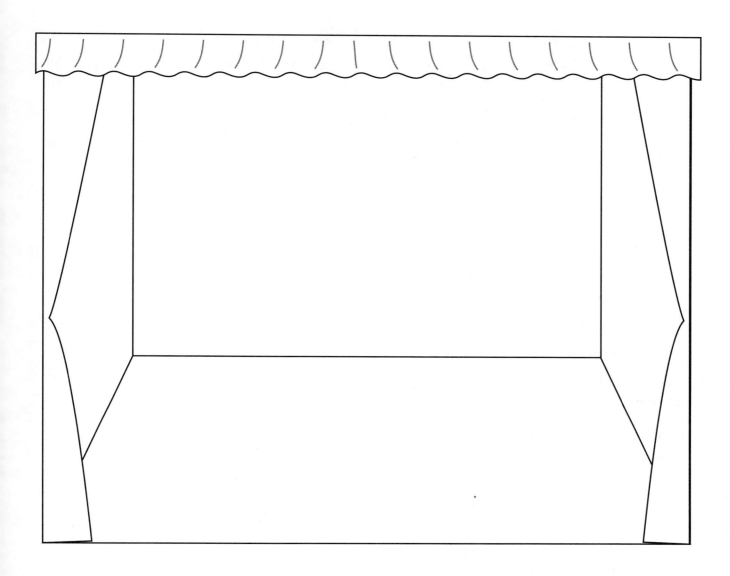

How I want the audience to feel watching this scene: _____

_____

_____

_____

_____

_____

_____

_____

The Ghost speaks

Enter GHOST and HAMLET.

HAMLET:	Whither wilt thou lead me? Speak, I'll go no further.
GHOST:	Mark me.
HAMLET:	I will.
GHOST:	My hour is almost come
	When I to sulph'rous and tormenting flames
	Must render up myself.
HAMLET:	Alas, poor ghost.
GHOST:	Pity me not, but lend thy serious hearing
	To what I shall unfold.
HAMLET:	Speak, I am bound to hear.
GHOST:	So art thou to revenge when thou shalt hear.
HAMLET:	What?
GHOST:	I am thy father's spirit,
	Doom'd for a certain term to walk the night,
	And for the day confin'd to fast in fires,
	Till the foul crimes done in my days of nature
	Are burnt and purg'd away. But that I am forbid
	To tell the secrets of my prison-house,
	I could a tale unfold whose lightest word
	Would harrow up thy soul, freeze thy young blood,
	Make thy two eyes like stars start from their spheres,
	Thy knotted and combined locks to part,
	And each particular hair to stand an end
	Like quills upon the fretful porpentine.

But this eternal blazon must not be
To ears of flesh and blood. List, list, O list!
If thou didst ever thy dear father love –

HAMLET: O God!

GHOST: Revenge his foul and most unnatural murder.

HAMLET: Murder!

GHOST: Murder most foul, as in the best it is,
But this most foul, strange and unnatural.

HAMLET: Haste me to know't, that I with wings as swift
As meditation or the thoughts of love
May sweep to my revenge.

GHOST: I find thee apt.
And duller shouldst thou be than the fat weed
That roots itself in ease on Lethe wharf,
Wouldst thou not stir in this. Now, Hamlet, hear.
'Tis given out that, sleeping in my orchard,
A serpent stung me – so the whole ear of Denmark
Is by a forged process of my death
Rankly abus'd – but know, thou noble youth,
The serpent that did sting thy father's life
Now wears his crown.

HAMLET: O my prophetic soul! My uncle!

From *Hamlet* by William Shakespeare

The Ghost speaks, annotated version

Enter GHOST *and* HAMLET.

HAMLET: Whither wilt thou lead me? Speak, I'll go no further.

listen to me ——

GHOST: Mark me.

HAMLET: I will.

the ghost
can only
appear at
night
because
during the
day he is
confined to
purgatory ——

GHOST: My **hour** is almost come   *daybreak*

When I to sulph'rous and tormenting flames

Must **render up** myself.   *go back*

HAMLET: Alas, poor ghost.

GHOST: Pity me not, but lend thy serious hearing

To what I shall unfold.

I have no
choice but
to hear ——

HAMLET: Speak, I am bound to hear.

GHOST: So art thou to revenge when thou shalt hear.

HAMLET: What?

GHOST: I am thy father's spirit,

Doom'd for a certain **term** to walk the night,   *time*

And for the day confin'd to fast in fires,

Till the foul **crimes** done in my **days of nature**   *sins / whilst
alive*

Are burnt and purg'd away. But that I am forbid

are
forgiven

To tell the secrets of my prison-house,

the ghost is
not allowed
to tell
Hamlet
what it is
like in
purgatory –
but if he
could,
Hamlet
would be
terrified

I could a tale unfold whose lightest word

Would harrow up thy soul, freeze thy young blood,

Make thy two eyes like stars start from their spheres,

Thy knotted and combined locks to part,

And each particular hair to stand an end

Like quills upon the **fretful porpentine**.

timid
porcupine

But this **eternal blazon** must not be

description
of eternity –
life after
death

To ears of flesh and blood. **List, list, O list!**

listen

If thou didst ever thy dear father love –

HAMLET: O God!

GHOST: Revenge his foul and most unnatural murder.

murder is
always
horrible,
but this was
especially
foul
because he
was killed
by his
brother

HAMLET: Murder!

GHOST: Murder most foul, as in the best it is,

But this most foul, strange and unnatural.

HAMLET: **Haste me to know't**, that I with wings as swift

tell me quickly

Hamlet is promising to act at the speed of thought

As meditation or the thoughts of love

May sweep to my revenge.

GHOST: I find thee apt.

And duller shouldst thou be than the fat weed

That roots itself in ease on **Lethe** wharf,

the river of forgetfulness in the Underworld

Wouldst thou not stir in this. Now, Hamlet, hear.

'**Tis given out** that, sleeping in my orchard,

everyone has been told

A serpent stung me – so the whole ear of Denmark

Is by a **forged process of my death**

a false account of how he died

Rankly abus'd – but know, thou noble youth,

The serpent that did sting thy father's life

Now wears his crown.

Hamlet has not actually prophesied that his uncle killed his father, but he has suspected that his uncle is up to no good

HAMLET: O my prophetic soul! My uncle!

From *Hamlet* by William Shakespeare

Playscripts

Learning target

On completion of this unit the children should be able to:

1 ➤➤ prepare a short section of story as a script, e.g. using stage directions, location/setting

Before you start

Background knowledge

The children have studied the layout and conventions of scripting (see Links to other units) from the starting point of looking at extracts from published plays. In this Unit, the emphasis is on turning a story extract into a playscript, using their knowledge of dialogue, character, stage directions and setting. Time should be allowed for the children to perform their plays.

Three copymasters are provided with story extracts from long-established authors. Different groups can work on each of these extracts to allow for variety when the scripts are performed. Alternatively, you may like to choose extracts from the class reader for the children to work on.

Resources for Session 1

Copymaster 47 The Wolves of Willoughby Chase
Copymaster 48 The Phantom Tollbooth
Copymaster 49 The Railway Children
Copymaster 50 Planning framework

Links to other units

Learning Targets: Fiction and Poetry Years 3 and 4
Year 3 Term 1 Unit 2: Dialogue
Year 4 Term 1 Unit 2: Playscripts
Learning Targets: Fiction and Poetry Years 5 and 6
Year 5 Term 1 Unit 3: Playscripts

Assessment indicators

* Can the children use their knowledge of scripting conventions to produce a script based on a story extract?
* Can they practise and perform their script?

Teaching the session

Session 1 ➊

Introduction 　　　20+ min

▨ This introductory session can be approached in two ways:

1 Explain to the children that they are going to prepare a short prose extract as a playscript. The work will be done in groups and the final script will be performed to the class. Discuss what the children can remember about:

* how a playscript looks on the page and how this differs from a story
* the differences between reading a story and seeing it acted on the stage or television
* the terms – dialogue, stage direction, setting, props, character, plot.

2 If you feel the children need more support then use *Learning Targets: Fiction and poetry Years 5 and 6* Year 5 Term 1 Unit 3 as revision. **Copymaster 9 Lady Windermere's Fan** will remind them of the layout of a script and how different type faces are used for the characters' names, stage directions and dialogue. A class discussion about staging conventions can be based on this.

Preparing the script 　　　30+ min

⦿ In groups, the children will work on one of the following story extracts:

Copymaster 47 The Wolves of Willoughby Chase – 3 female characters

Copymaster 48 The Phantom Tollbooth – 6 characters plus dog

Copymaster 49 The Railway Children – 2 female and 1 male character

Copymaster 50 Planning framework will give the children a starting point to note the number of characters and their names, write notes on the setting and draw it as it would appear on stage.

The children should work in draft form at first. One group member should be elected as the scribe and write the script that has been agreed on through group discussion.

Be on hand to monitor the work in progress. Children do not usually have much difficulty with transcribing the dialogue from a story to a script but you may find it very light on stage directions. With some groups you may find it appropriate to suggest that extra dialogue is added. The audience will not have the narrative parts of the story and may need the characters to say more so that they understand what is going on.

Suggest that each child thinks carefully about the character they are going to play:

- What sort of person is that character?
- How will he/she say things?
- What sort of movements or gestures will that character make during the play?

When a neat copy has been achieved, it is useful if it can be photocopied for the other group members to avoid endless handwritten copying. The children could highlight their lines using coloured pens to make the script easier to follow.

For the performance you, or one of the group members, can read the potted summary of the story so far from the top of each copymaster.

Summary

 A discussion of the script/performance can take place after individual group performances or when all the groups working on the same story extract have performed.

Encourage the children to be sensitive in their appraisal of the performances, concentrating on the positive aspects. They should, however, note places where they:

- found it difficult to follow the story line – should more dialogue have been added?
- felt that a character or characters did not 'do' much – should more stage directions be written in?

The story extracts can be photocopied and mounted; the children's playscripts can then be displayed around the relevant extract.

104

The Wolves of Willoughby Chase

In this extract from the story, Miss Slighcarp is posing as a governess. She is taken on by Bonnie and Sylvia's parents and is looking after the children while their parents are away.

The governess, who had been examining some books on the shelves, swung round with equal abruptness. She seemed astonished to see them.

'Where have you been?' she demanded angrily, after an instant's pause.

'Why,' Sylvia faltered, 'merely in the next room, Miss Slighcarp.'

But Bonnie, with choking utterance, demanded, 'Why are you wearing my mother's dress?'

Sylvia had observed that Miss Slighcarp had on a draped gown of old gold velvet with ruby buttons, far grander than the grey twill she had worn the day before.

'Don't speak to me in that way, miss!' retorted Miss Slighcarp in a rage. 'You have been spoiled all your life, but we shall soon see who is going to be mistress now. Go to your place and sit down. Do not speak until you are spoken to.'

Bonnie paid not the slightest attention. 'Who said you could wear my mother's best gown?' she repeated. Sylvia, alarmed, had slipped into her place at the table, but Bonnie, reckless with indignation, stood in front of the governess, glaring at her.

'Everything in this house was left entirely to my personal disposition,' Miss Slighcarp said coldly.

'But not her clothes! Not to wear! How *dare* you? Take it off at once! It's no better than stealing!'

Two white dents had appeared on either side of Miss Slighcarp's nostrils.

'Another word and it's the dark cupboard and bread-and-water for you, miss,' she said fiercely.

'I don't care what you say!' Bonnie stamped her foot. 'Take off my mother's dress!'

Miss Slighcarp boxed Bonnie's ears. Bonnie seized Miss Slighcarp's wrists. In the confusion a bottle of ink was knocked off the table, spilling a long blue trail down the gold velvet skirt. Miss Slighcarp uttered an exclamation of fury.

'Insolent, ungovernable child! You shall suffer for this!' With iron strength she thrust Bonnie into a closet containing crayons, globes and exercise books, and turned the key on her. Then she swept from the room.

Sylvia remained seated, aghast, for half a second. Then she ran to the cupboard door – but alas! Miss Slighcarp had taken the key with her.

'Bonnie! Bonnie! Are you all right? It's I, Sylvia.'

She could hear bitter sobs.

'Don't cry, Bonnie, please don't cry. I'll run after her and beg her to let you out. I dare say she will, once she has reflected. She can't have known it was your mother's *favourite* gown.'

From *The Wolves of Willoughby Chase* by Joan Aiken

The Phantom Tollbooth

Milo is not very keen on going to school. In fact, he thinks learning is a waste of time. One day he is given a turnpike tollbooth as a present. When he goes inside the tollbooth he arrives in all sorts of strange places with very peculiar people. In this adventure, he, and Tock the dog, find themselves in the Kingdom of Dictionopolis where all the words in the world are grown.

'I wonder what the market will be like,' thought Milo as they drove through the gate; but before there was time for an answer they had driven into an immense square crowded with long lines of stalls heaped with merchandise and decorated in gaily coloured bunting. Overhead a large banner proclaimed:

WELCOME TO THE WORD MARKET

And, from across the square, five very tall, thin gentlemen regally dressed in silks and satins, plumed hats, and buckled shoes rushed up to the car, stopped short, mopped five brows, caught five breaths, unrolled five parchments, and began talking in turn.

'Greetings!'

'Salutations!'

'Welcome!'

'Good afternoon!'

'Hello!'

Milo nodded his head, and they went on, reading from their scrolls.

'By order of Azaz the Unabridged –'

'King of Dictionopolis –'

'Monarch of letters –'

'Emperor of phrases, sentences and miscellaneous figures of speech –'

'We offer you the hospitality of our kingdom,'

'Country,'

'Nation,'

'State,'

'Commonwealth,'

'Realm,'

'Empire,'

'Palatinate,'

'Principality.'

'Do all those words mean the same thing?' gasped Milo.

'Of course.'

'Certainly.'

'Precisely.'

'Exactly.'

'Yes,' they replied in order.

'Well, then,' said Milo, not understanding why each one said the same thing in a slightly different way, 'wouldn't it be simpler to use just one? It would certainly make more sense.'

'Nonsense.'

'Ridiculous.'

'Fantastic.'

'Absurd.'

'Bosh,' they chorused again, and continued:

'We're not interested in making sense; it's not our job,' scolded the first.

'Besides,' explained the second, 'one word is as good as another – so why not use them all?'

'Then you don't have to choose which one is right,' advised the third.

'Besides,' sighed the fourth, 'if one is right, then ten are ten times as right.'

'Obviously you don't know who we are,' sneered the fifth. And they presented themselves one by one as:

'The Duke of Definition.'

'The Minister of Meaning.'

'The Earl of Essence.'

'The Count of Connotation.'

'The Under-Secretary of Understanding.'

Milo acknowledged the introduction and, as Tock growled softly, the minister explained.

'We are the King's advisers, or, in more formal terms, his cabinet.'

'Cabinet,' recited the Duke: '(1) a small private room or closet, case with drawers, etc., for keeping valuables or displaying curiosities; (2) council room for chief ministers of state; (3) a body of official advisers to the chief executive of a nation.'

'You see,' continued the minister, bowing thankfully to the duke, 'Dictionopolis is the place where all the words in the world come from. They're grown right here in our orchards.'

'I didn't know that words grew on trees,' said Milo timidly.

From *The Phantom Tollbooth* by Norton Juster

The Railway Children

Three children and their mother have moved to the country from London and live by a railway line. In this extract the children are near the railway picking cherries when trees, earth and stones slide down the bank and fall onto the railway track.

'Look what a great mound it's made!' said Bobbie.

'Yes, it's right across the down line,' said Phyllis.

'That'll take some sweeping up,' said Bobbie.

'Yes,' said Peter slowly. He was still leaning on the fence.

'Yes,' he said again, still more slowly.

Then he stood upright.

'The 11.29 down hasn't gone by yet. We must let them know at the station, or there'll be a most frightful accident.'

'Let's run,' said Bobbie, and began.

But Peter cried, 'Come back!' and looked at Mother's watch. He was very prompt and businesslike, and his face looked whiter than they had ever seen it.

'No time,' he said; 'it's ten miles away, and it's past eleven.'

'Couldn't we,' suggested Phyllis, breathlessly, 'couldn't we climb up a telegraph post and do something to the wires?'

'We don't know how,' said Peter.

'They do it in war,' said Phyllis; 'I know I've heard of it.'

'They only *cut* them, silly,' said Peter, 'and that doesn't do any good. And we couldn't cut them even if we got up, and we couldn't get up. If we had anything red, we could go down on the line and wave it.'

'But the train wouldn't see us till it got round the corner, and then it could see the mound just as well as us,' said Phyllis; 'better, because it's much bigger than us.'

'If we only had something red,' Peter repeated, 'we could go round the corner and wave to the train.'

'We might wave, anyway.'

'They'd only think it was just *us*, as usual. We've waved so often before. Anyway, let's get down.'

They got down the steep stairs. Bobbie was pale and shivering. Peter's face looked thinner than usual. Phyllis was red-faced and damp with anxiety.

'Oh, how hot I am!' she said; 'and I thought it was going to be cold; I wish we hadn't put on our – ' she stopped short, and then ended in quite a different tone – our flannel petticoats.'

Bobbie turned at the bottom of the stairs.

'Oh, yes,' she cried, '*they're* red!'

From *The Railway Children* by E. Nesbit

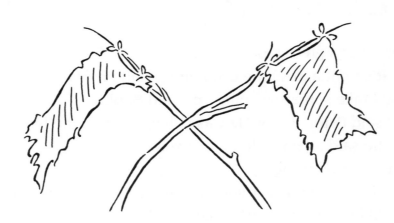

Planning framework

Story extract:

Characters:

Setting:

How the stage should look:

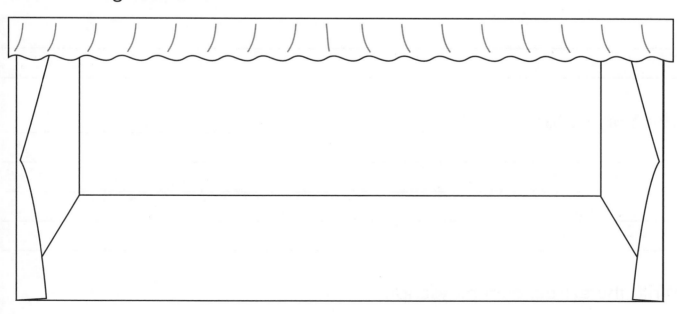

Choose a short extract from a story you have recently read and enjoyed. The extract must have two or more characters speaking to each other. Use the space below to make notes on:

- characters
- the story so far ...
- setting
- stage directions

Characters: _____

_____

_____

_____

_____

Setting: _____

_____

_____

_____

_____

Stage directions: _____

_____

_____

_____

_____

The story so far: _____

_____

_____

_____

_____

Write the extract as a playscript.

YEAR 6 TERM 2

Focus

In this section the children will be given the opportunity to:

1 investigate, discuss and write humorous verse
2 investigate how authors build-up suspense
3 write own endings to an episode where suspense is built and has to be continued.

Content

Unit 1: Humorous poems
Unit 2: Building suspense

Extract list

Carroll, Lewis: 'Jabberwocky'
Cope, Wendy: 'Kenneth'
Dahl, Roald: 'The Centipede's Song'
Falkner, J. Meade: *Moonfleet*
Milligan, Spike: 'A Thousand Hairy Savages'
Nash, Ogden: 'Celery'
Rieu, E.V.: 'Sir Smasham Uppe'

Assessment

Assessment Copymasters 58–9 are at the end of the section.

Copymaster 58 Writing a humorous poem gives the children a variety of starting points for poetry writing.

Copymaster 59 Writing a suspense story gives the children starting points for writing a story which relies upon suspense.

Curriculum Planner
National Literacy Strategy Planner

This chart shows you how to find activities by unit to resource your term's requirements for text level work on fiction and poetry. The Learning Targets closely follow the structure of the fiction and poetry requirements for the term in the National Literacy Strategy document (pages 52–53). A few of the requirements are not covered.

YEAR 6   Term 2

Range

Fiction and poetry:

* longer established stories and novels selected from more than one genre; e.g. mystery, humour, sci-fi, historical, fantasy worlds, etc.
* to study and compare; range of poetic forms

TEXT LEVEL WORK

COMPREHENSION AND COMPOSITION

Reading comprehension

Pupils should be taught:

4 to investigate humorous verse:
   * how poets play with meanings;
   * nonsense words and how meaning can be made of them;
   * where the appeal lies; Unit 1

8 to analyse the success of texts and writers in evoking particular responses in the reader, e.g. where suspense is well built; Unit 2

Writing composition

Pupils should be taught:

10 to use different genres as models to write, e.g. short extracts, sequels, additional episodes, alternative endings, using appropriate conventions, language; Unit 2

Humorous poems

Learning target

On completion of this unit the children should be able to:

1 ➤➤ investigate humorous verse:
- how poets play with meanings
- nonsense words and how meaning can be made of them
- where the appeal lies.

Before you start

Background knowledge

There are two difficulties with the seemingly simple statement 'investigate humorous verse'. Firstly, the range of poetry of this type is vast, and secondly, 'humour' is very subjective. In preparation, ask the children to think of poems which have amused them for discussion in the first session.

This wide category of poetry is more easily handled if there is a thematic link.

Session 1 deals with food, Session 2 with people and Session 3 with the use of nonsense language.

Resources for Session 1

Copymaster 52 Food is funny!

Resources for Session 2

Copymaster 53 Kenneth
Copymaster 54 Sir Smasham Uppe

Resources for Session 3

Copymaster 55 The Centipede's Song
Copymaster 56 Jabberwocky

Links to other units

Learning Targets: Fiction and Poetry Years 3 and 4
Year 3 Term 1 Unit 3: Poetry writing
Year 3 Term 3 Unit 4: Playing with language
Year 4 Term 1 Unit 3: Poetry writing
Learning Targets: Fiction and Poetry Years 5 and 6
Year 5 Term 3 Unit 2: Performance poetry

Assessment indicators

- Can the children read and discuss humorous poetry with a view to articulating the source of the humour?
- Can they say why they do or do not find a particular poem funny?
- Can they write their own humorous verse?

Teaching the sessions

Session 1 ①

Introduction 20-30min

Spend some time at the beginning of the session discussing any humorous poetry which the children have brought in. If the poems are fairly short, some can be read to the class and discussed:
- Do all the children think it is funny?
- Can they say why?
- Can any children who are not amused explain why?

Discuss what reaction a humorous poem provokes:
- Is it only humorous if the reader laughs out loud?
- Do people simply smile at a humorous poem?

Explain that you are going to look at several humorous poems to do with food and eating. Explore with the children why they think the subject of food can be made amusing, before looking at the poems. Is there any particular food the children can think of as funny? Spaghetti is often suggested because it looks like worms and people are often very messy when they eat it. Keep a list of 'funny foods' to remind the children when they come to write their own poems.

Is it funny? 15-20min

Give each group **Copymaster 52 Food is funny!**, which has a variety of humorous poems, linked by the theme of food. In group discussion they should consider each poem in turn and decide:

- Is it funny?
- Why is it amusing?
- Why isn't it amusing?

This may appear to be a rather sterile, analytical exercise but it is trying to get the children to analyse the *source* of humour, e.g.

- a humorous situation
- a humorous character
- a humorous way of playing with words.

Stress that the group does not have to come to a consensus. Each individual is entitled to his/her own views as long as they are backed up by reasons.

Summary ⌗ 10-15 min

Each group should report back to the rest of the class as to how funny they found the poems. This is a good opportunity to give the children useful words and phrases linked to discussion outcomes, e.g. unanimous, opinion was divided and we could/couldn't reach a consensus.

Session 2 ❶

Introduction ⌗ 10-15 min

In this session the children are going to examine character and situation as a source of humour. They can probably best relate this to television comedy where the central character often finds him/herself in ridiculous situations; the combination of the situation and how the character responds to it being the source of the humour. Discuss what the children find funny on television and why.

Two poems ⌗ 20-30 min

In groups the children should read and discuss **Copymaster 53 Kenneth** and **Copymaster 54 Sir Smasham Uppe**.

They should investigate:

- if and why they find the poems funny
- what the source of the humour is
- which poem they find more amusing and why.

If time permits, each group could choose one of the poems to prepare and perform for the rest of the class. The group performance should concentrate on bringing out the humour of the poem.

Summary ⌗ 10-15 min

Each group should share its findings with the rest of the class.

Session 3 ❶

Introduction ⌗ 20-25 min

In this session the children are going to examine the words used by poets as a source of humour. Give each child **Copymaster 55 The Centipede's Song** and read it through with the class. This is a gentle introduction to the use of made-up words and extends the theme of food from Session 1. Discuss if and why the children find the poem funny, paying particular attention to the 'made-up' words: 'dandyprats', 'mudburgers', 'slobbages', 'doodlebugs' and 'wampfish'.

Jabberwocky ⌗ 30+ min

Give each group **Copymaster 56 Jabberwocky**. You can tackle this as a whole class discussion or allow the children to come to it 'cold' in a group situation. They should discuss:

- if and why they find it funny
- if they understood what was going on despite the strange vocabulary
- if the strange vocabulary adds to the humour.

Let each group replace the 'made-up' words with real words of their own which they think reflect the original meaning.

Summary ⌗ 15-20 min

Investigate the groups' findings through class discussion and 'translate' the poem using the best suggestions for each of the 'made-up' words.

My own humorous poem ⌗ 30+ min

Using any of the poems as a model the children should now attempt to write their own humorous poem. If they choose to write on the theme of food, remind them of the funny foods you discussed in Session 1. You need to be on hand to help with the editing process. When the poems are complete they can be neatly copied or word processed, illustrated and displayed.

Food is funny!

52

Celery

Celery, raw,
Develops the jaw,
But celery, stewed,
Is more quietly chewed.
        Ogden Nash

Peas

I always eat peas with honey,
I've done it all my life,
They do taste kind of funny
But it keeps them on the knife.
        Anon

If You Should Meet a Crocodile

If you should meet a crocodile,
    Don't take a stick and poke him;
Ignore the welcome in his smile,
    Be careful not to stroke him.
For as he sleeps upon the Nile,
    He thinner gets and thinner;
But whene'er you meet a crocodile
    He's ready for his dinner.
            Anon

There was a Young Lady from Ickenham

There was a young lady from Ickenham
Who went on a bus trip to Twickenham
She drank too much beer
Which made her feel queer
So she took off her boots and was sick-in-em.
            Anon

A Thousand Hairy Savages

A thousand hairy savages
Sitting down to lunch
Gobble gobble glup glup
Munch munch munch
        Spike Milligan

Kenneth

Who was too fond of bubble-gum and met an untimely end

The chief defect of Kenneth Plumb
Was chewing too much bubble-gum.
He chewed away with all his might,
Morning, evening, noon and night.
Even (oh, it makes you weep)
Blowing bubbles in his sleep.

He simply couldn't get enough!
His face was covered with the stuff.
As for his teeth – oh, what a sight!
It was a wonder he could bite.
His loving mother and his dad
Both remonstrated with the lad.

Ken repaid them for the trouble
By blowing yet another bubble.

'Twas no joke. It isn't funny
Spending all your pocket money
On the day's supply of gum –
Sometimes Kenny felt quite glum.
As he grew, so did his need –
There seemed no limit to his greed:
At ten he often put away
Ninety-seven packs a day.

Then at last he went too far –
Sitting in his father's car,
Stuffing gum without a pause,
Found that he had jammed his jaws.
He nudged his dad and pointed to
The mouthful that he couldn't chew.
'Well, spit it out if you can't chew it!'
Ken shook his head. He couldn't do it.

Before long he began to groan –
The gum was solid as a stone
Dad took him to a builder's yard;
They couldn't help. It was too hard.

They called a doctor and he said,
'This silly boy will soon be dead.
His mouth's so full of bubble-gum
No nourishment can reach his tum.'

Remember Ken and please do not
Go buying too much you-know-what.

Wendy Cope

Sir Smasham Uppe

Good afternoon, Sir Smasham Uppe!
We're having tea: do take a cup!
Sugar and milk? Now let me see –
Two lumps, I think? … Good gracious me!
The silly thing slipped off your knee!
Pray don't apologize, old chap:
A very trivial mishap!
So clumsy of you? How absurd!
My dear Sir Smasham, not a word!
Now, do sit down and have another,
And tell us all about your brother –
You know, the one who broke his head.
Is the poor fellow still in bed? –
A chair – allow me, sir! … Great Scott!
That *was* a nasty smash! Eh, what?
Oh, not at all: the chair was old –
Queen Anne, or so we have been told.
We've got at least a dozen more:
Just leave the pieces on the floor.
I want you to admire our view:
Come nearer to the window, do;
And look how beautiful … Tut, tut!
You didn't see that it was shut?
I hope you are not badly cut!
Not hurt? A fortunate escape!
Amazing! Not a single scrape!
And now, if you have finished tea,
I fancy you might like to see
A little thing or two I've got.
That china plate? Yes, worth a lot:
A beauty too … Ah, there it goes!
I trust it didn't hurt your toes?
Your elbow brushed it off the shelf?
Of course: I've done the same myself.
And now, my dear Sir Smasham – Oh,
You surely don't intend to go?
You *must* be off? Well, come again,
So glad you're fond of porcelain.

E.V. Rieu

The Centipede's Song

'I've eaten many strange and scrumptious dishes in my time,
Like jellied gnats and dandyprats and earwigs cooked in slime,
And mice with rice – they're really nice
When roasted in their prime.
(But don't forget to sprinkle them with just a pinch of grime.)

'I've eaten fresh mudburgers by the greatest cooks there are,
And scrambled dregs and stinkbugs' eggs and hornets stewed in tar,
And pails of snails and lizards' tails,
And beetles by the jar.
(A beetle is improved by just a splash of vinegar.)

'I often eat boiled slobbages. They're grand when served beside
Minced doodlebugs and curried slugs. And have you ever tried
Mosquitoes' toes and wampfish roes
Most delicately fried?
(The only trouble is they disagree with my inside.)

'I'm mad for crispy wasp-stings on a piece of buttered toast,
And pickled spines on porcupines. And then a gorgeous roast
Of dragon's flesh, well hung, not fresh –
It costs a pound at most,
(And comes to you in barrels if you order it by
      post.)

'I crave the tasty tentacles of octopi for tea
I like hot-dogs, I LOVE hot-frogs, and surely
      you'll agree
A plate of soil with engine oil's
A super recipe.
(I hardly need to mention that it's practically
      free.)

'For dinner on my birthday shall I tell you what
      I chose:
Hot noodles made from poodles on a slice of garden hose –
And a rather smelly jelly
Made of armadillo's toes.
(The jelly is delicious, but you have to hold your nose.)
…'

From James and the Giant Peach by Roald Dahl

Jabberwocky

'Twas brillig, and the slithy toves
    Did gyre and gimble in the wabe;
All mimsy were the borogroves,
    And the mome raths outgrabe.

'Beware the Jabberwock, my son!
    The jaws that bite, the claws that catch!
Beware the Jubjub bird, and shun
    The frumious Bandersnatch!'

He took his vorpal sword in hand:
    Long time the manxome foe he sought –
So rested he by the Tumtum tree,
    And stood awhile in thought.

And, as in uffish thought he stood,
    The Jabberwock, with eyes of flame,
Came whiffling through the tulgy wood,
    And burbled as it came!

One, two! One, two! And through and through
    The vorpal blade went snicker-snack!
He left it dead, and with its head
    He went galumphing back.

'And hast thou slain the Jabberwock?
    Come to my arms, my beamish boy!
O frabjous day! Callooh! Callay!'
    He chortled in his joy.

'Twas brillig, and the slithy toves
    Did gyre and gimble in the wabe:
All mimsy were the borogroves,
    And the mome raths outgrabe.

Lewis Carroll

Building suspense

Learning targets

On completion of this unit the children should be able to:

1 ➡➡ analyse the success of texts and writers in evoking particular responses in the reader, e.g. where suspense is well built

2 ➡➡ use different genres as models to write, e.g. short extracts, sequels, additional episodes, alternative endings, using appropriate conventions, language.

Before you start

Background knowledge

The aim of this unit is to give the children the opportunity to look at how suspense is created by a writer in a long established story. The copymaster extract is taken from *Moonfleet* by J. Meade Falkner and is a long piece which sees the suspense build-up from when John Trenchard, the narrator, first enters the vault to the moment where he realises he is not alone.

The activities for group and individual work can be adapted to suit an extract from the class reader if you prefer.

Resources for Session 1

Copymaster 57 Moonfleet

Assessment indicators

- Can the children chart the build-up of suspense in an episode from a story?
- Can they pick out words and phrases which create an atmosphere of suspense?
- Can they resolve a situation in a story which has reached a climax of suspense?

Teaching the sessions

Session 1 ➊ ➋

Introduction   20–30 min

 Give each child **Copymaster 57 Moonfleet**, and read it through with them. Before the children work in groups to investigate the build-up of suspense in the extract, a class session should take place to ensure literal understanding of this fairly difficult text. The children need to understand:

1 what has happened in the story before John enters the vault:
- from the introduction
  - John lives in Moonfleet.
  - The vault under the church contains generations of the dead Mohunes.
  - One of the dead Mohunes, known as Blackbeard, is said to have died knowing the whereabouts of a large diamond.
  - Blackbeard is said to haunt the vault.
- from the text
  - One Sunday morning, shortly before John's

visit to the vault, sounds had been heard coming from it.
  - The vault had been flooded.
  - One villager, called Ratsey, had put around the story that the noises from the vault were made by Blackbeard.
  - Another villager, called Elzevir, did not normally attend church but was there the morning the noises were heard.
  - John had stumbled across both Ratsey and Elzevir in the churchyard, Ratsey was listening with his ear to the vault wall.
  - John had seen strange lights in the churchyard after dark.
  - Cracky Jones had been found dead in the churchyard.

2 what happens when John is in the vault:
  - He finds coffins and casks of liquor.
  - He realises the vault is where those smuggling liquor into the country, without paying tax, store their contraband.
  - He discovers it was the casks knocking together that made the strange noises that

were heard on Sunday morning when the vault was flooded.

–   He reasons that both Ratsey and Elzevir are involved with the smuggling and Ratsey's tale of Blackbeard was just a story to frighten anyone away who might get too curious.

–   Having failed to find the diamond he is just about to leave when the church bell strikes midnight.

–   He hears another noise and soon deduces that people are entering the vault.

–   He realises he must not be discovered and hides himself between the wall and a coffin just as the lights of torches are approaching the vault.

Explain to the children that these are the events before and during John's visit to the vault but, listed in this way, they are not particularly exciting, nor do they affect the reader as the author intended.

What do the children understand by the terms 'suspense' and 'being on the edge of one's seat'? Can they give you specific examples from their reading or from television and films?

Explain that a straightforward list of events can be presented in such a way as to put the reader on 'the edge of their seat'.

Building suspense

In groups, the children should discuss how the author has built-up suspense from the moment John enters the vault to when he has to hide. They should look for specific events which put the reader at ease, and specific events which make the reader anxious and discuss the words and phrases used to express this.

Events which put the reader at ease:

*   John describes the vault in some detail which makes it seem like a less threatening place.
*   Instead of being a haunted, forbidding place, it is a place where a very human activity, i.e. smuggling, is going on.
*   The strange noises are explained.
*   The story about Blackbeard is explained.
*   The strange lights in the churchyard are explained.

Events which make the reader uneasy:

*   The clock in the tower strikes midnight.
*   The stillness of the vault is broken by another noise.

*   John realises the noise is that of people talking.
*   He will be caught in a trap with no means of escape.
*   He remembers the death of Cracky Jones in the churchyard.
*   He hears someone jump down into the hole which leads to the vault.
*   He has no choice but to hide behind a coffin.
*   He bangs his head and is dazed.
*   There is only a thin rotten plank between him and a corpse.
*   The flickering of torch light comes nearer.

Words and phrases:

*   'my heart beat very fiercely'
*   'dreadful sounds'
*   'evil lurking in the dark corners'
*   'it was a sad thing to be cabined with so many dead men'
*   'the clock in the tower struck midnight'
*   'never was ghostly hour sounded in more ghostly place'
*   'the awful stillness of the vault was broken'
*   'I knew it was the sound of voices talking'
*   'what a minute was that to me!'
*   'I can recall the anguish of it'
*   'clammy sweat upon my face'
*   'it was the anguish of the rabbit ... and how men *said* he had met Blackbeard in the night'
*   the whole of the final paragraph.

Summary

Discuss the groups' findings and investigate why, in the beginning of the extract, the author allows the reader to know that all the ghostly elements are easily explained away? (To build suspense an author may use the technique of lulling the reader into a false sense of security.) In this extract the reader may expect a ghostly visitation of Blackbeard. That expectation is not fulfilled but the narrator finds himself confronting an equal, if not greater, danger.

What happens next?

The children can plan and draft an ending to this episode. The two possible outcomes are that John is discovered or he escapes undetected. Explain to the children that whichever one they choose they should continue the element of suspense and not resolve John's difficult situation too quickly or easily.

Moonfleet

John Trenchard is a young boy who lives in the village of Moonfleet. In a vault under the church are buried generations of the Mohune family, one of whom was known as Blackbeard. Rumour has it that a large diamond disappeared when Blackbeard died. John is sure that it is buried in the vault and decides to go down and see if he can find it, despite the fact that some say Blackbeard does not rest easy in his grave!

… before the light had well time to fall on things, I knew that I was underneath the church, and that this chamber was none other than the Mohune Vault.

It was a large room, much larger, I think, than the schoolroom where Mr Glennie taught us, but not near so high, being only some nine feet from floor to roof. I say floor, though in reality there was none, but only a bottom of soft wet sand; and when I stepped down on to it my heart beat very fiercely, for I remembered what manner of place I was entering, and the dreadful sounds which had issued from it that Sunday morning so short a time before. I satisfied myself that there was nothing evil lurking in the dark corners, or nothing visible at least, and then began to look round and note what was to be seen. Walls and roof were stone, and at one end was a staircase closed by a great flat stone at top – that same stone which I had often seen, with a ring in it, in the floor of the church above. All round the sides were stone shelves, with divisions between them like great bookcases, but instead of books there were the coffins of the Mohunes. Yet these lay only at the sides, and in the middle of the room was something very different, for here were stacked scores of casks, kegs and runlets, from a storage butt that might hold thirty gallons down to a breaker that held only one. They were marked all of them in white paint on the end with

figures and letters, that doubtless set forth the quality to those that understood. Here indeed was a discovery, and instead of picking up at the end of the passage a little brass or silver casket which had only to be opened to show Blackbeard's diamond gleaming inside, I had stumbled on the Mohunes' vault, and found it to be nothing but a cellar of gentlemen of the contraband, for surely good liquor would never be stored in so shy a place if it ever had paid excise.

As I walked round this stack of casks my foot struck sharply on the edge of a butt, which must have been near empty, and straightway came from it the same hollow booming sound (only fainter) which had so frightened us in church that Sunday morning. So it was the casks, and not the coffins, that had been knocking one against another; and I was pleased with myself, remembering how I had reasoned that coffin-wood could never give that booming sound.

It was plain enough that the whole place had been under water: the floor was still muddy, and the green and sweating walls showed the flood mark within two feet of the roof; there was a wisp or two of fine seaweed that had somehow got in, and a small crab was still alive and scuttled across the corner, yet the coffins were but little disturbed. They lay on the shelves in rows, one above the other, and numbered twenty-three in all: most were in lead, and so could never float, but of those in wood some were turned slantways in their niches, and one had floated right away and been left on the floor upside down in a corner when the waters went back.

First I fell to wondering as to whose cellar this was, and how so much liquor could have been brought in with secrecy; and how it was I had never seen anything of the contraband-men, though it was clear that they had made this flat tomb the entrance to their storehouse, as I had made it my seat. And then I remembered how Ratsey had tried to scare me with talk of Blackbeard; and how Elzevir, who had never been seen at church before, was there the Sunday of the noises; and how he had looked ill at ease whenever the noise came, though he was bold as a lion; and how I had tripped upon him and Ratsey in the churchyard; and how Master Ratsey lay with his ear to the wall: and putting all these things together and casting them up, I thought that Elzevir and Ratsey knew as much as any about this hiding-place. These reflections gave me more courage, for I considered that the tales of Blackbeard walking or digging among the graves had been set afloat to keep those that were not wanted from the place, and guessed now that when I saw the light moving in the churchyard that night I went to fetch Dr Hawkins, it was no corpse-candle, but a lantern of smugglers running a cargo.

Then, having settled these important matters, I began to turn over in my mind how to get at the treasure; and herein was much cast down, for in this place was neither casket nor diamond, but only coffins and double-Hollands. So it was that, having no better plan, I set to work to see whether I could learn anything from the coffins themselves; but with little success, for the lead coffins had no names upon them, and on such of the wooden coffins as bore plates I found the writing to be Latin, and so rusted over that I could make nothing of it.

Soon I wished I had not come at all, considering that the diamond had vanished into air, and it was a sad thing to be cabined with so many dead men. It moved me, too, to see pieces of banners and funeral shields, and even shreds of wreaths that dear hearts had put there a century ago, now all ruined and rotten – some still clinging, water-sodden, to the coffins, and some trampled in the sand of the floor. I had spent some time in this bootless search, and was resolved to give up further inquiry and foot it home, when the clock in the tower struck midnight. Surely never was ghostly hour sounded in more ghostly place. Moonfleet peal was known over half the county, and the finest part of it was the clock bell. 'Twas said that in times past (when, perhaps, the chimes were rung more often than now) the voice of this bell had led safe home boats that were lost in the fog; and this night its clangour, mellow and profound, reached even to the vault. Bim-bom it went, bim-bom, twelve heavy thuds that shook the walls, twelve resonant echoes that followed, and then a purring and vibration of the air, so that the ear could not tell when it ended.

I was wrought up, perhaps, by the strangeness of the hour and place, and my hearing quicker than at other times, but before the tremor of the bell was quite passed away I knew there was some other sound in the air, and that the awful stillness of the vault was broken. At first I could not tell what this new sound was, nor whence it came, and now it seemed a little noise close by, and now a great noise in the distance. And then it grew nearer and more defined, and in a moment I knew it was the sound of voices talking. They must have been a long way off at first, and for a minute, that seemed as an age, they came no nearer. What a minute was that to me! Even now, so many years after, I can recall the anguish of it, and how I stood with ears pricked up, eyes starting, and a clammy sweat upon my face, waiting for those speakers to come. It was the anguish of the rabbit at the end of his burrow, with the ferret's eyes gleaming in the dark, and gun and lurcher waiting at the mouth of the hole. I was caught in a trap, and knew beside that contraband-men had a way of sealing prying eyes and stilling babbling tongues; and I remembered poor Cracky Jones found dead in the churchyard, and how men *said* he had met Blackbeard in the night.

These were but the thoughts of a second, but the voices were nearer, and I heard a dull thud far up the passage, and knew that a man had jumped down from the churchyard into the hole. So I took a last stare round, agonizing to see if there was any way of escape; but the stone walls and roof were solid enough to crush me, and the stack of casks too closely packed to hide more than a rat. There was a man speaking now from the bottom of the hole to others in the churchyard, and then my eyes were led as by a loadstone to a great wooden coffin that lay by itself on the top shelf, a full six feet from the ground. When I saw that coffin I knew that I was respited, for, as I judged, there was space between it and the wall behind enough to contain my little carcass; and in a second I had put out the candle, scrambled up the shelves, half-stunned my senses with dashing my head against the roof, and squeezed my body betwixt wall and coffin. There I lay on one side with a thin and rotten plank between the dead man and me, dazed with the blow to my head, and breathing hard; while the glow of torches as they came down the passage reddened and flickered on the roof above.

From *Moonfleet* by J. Meade Falkner

Writing a humorous poem

Choose **one** of the following and write a humorous poem.

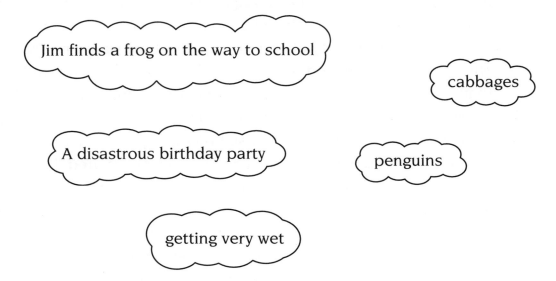

Jim finds a frog on the way to school

cabbages

A disastrous birthday party

penguins

getting very wet

- Your poem can be rhyming or non-rhyming.
- You may choose to write a poem about a funny character.
- You may choose to write about a funny situation.
- You may choose to write a cautionary tale.
- Work in draft and rewrite any parts of your poem which do not work.

Make notes on your first thoughts here: _____

_____

_____

_____

_____

_____

_____

_____

_____

Writing a suspense story

The following are starting points for a story that will keep readers 'on the edge of their seats':

An unkind farmer called Mr Brown keeps his dog chained up all day. Carl feels sorry for the dog and is determined to set it free. But can he do it without being caught?

Invitation to Danger!

I crept quietly into the deserted classroom...

The Storm

Two children are walking home from school through a wood. They take the same path every day but today, one of them notices that everything looks strange!

If only I hadn't found that old key...

The starting points are divided into three types:

- an explanation of the situation you must build your story on
- a title
- an opening line.

Choose one of the starting points and write a suspense story. Remember to plan plot, setting and characters.

YEAR 6 TERM 3

Focus

In this section the children will be given the opportunity to:

1 investigate and discuss poems linked by theme and form
2 write their own linked poems
3 investigate and write book blurbs
4 investigate and write book reviews.

Content

Unit 1: Linked poems
Unit 2: Book blurbs and reviews

Extract list

Agard, John: 'If I Could Only Take Home a Snowflake'
Andrew, Moira: 'Shower'
Cornish, Kay: 'Rain'
Matthews, Richard: 'Seasonal Haiku'
Moore, Lilian: 'Snowy Morning'

Assessment

Assessment Copymasters 70–1 are at the end of the section.

Copymaster 70 Writing three poems gives the children a variety of starting points for poetry writing.

Copymaster 71 Designing a book cover gives the children a starting point for designing a book cover and writing a book blurb.

Curriculum Planner
National Literacy Strategy Planner

This chart shows you how to find activities by unit to resource your term's requirements for text level work on fiction and poetry. The Learning Targets closely follow the structure of the fiction and poetry requirements for the term in the National Literacy Strategy document (pages 54–55). A few of the requirements are not covered.

YEAR 6 Term 3

Range

Fiction and poetry:

* comparison of work by significant children's authors and poets;
    (a) work by the same author
    (b) different authors' treatment of the same themes.

TEXT LEVEL WORK

COMPREHENSION AND COMPOSITION

Reading comprehension

Pupils should be taught:

2 to discuss how linked poems relate to one another by themes, format and repetition, e.g. cycle of poems about the seasons; Unit 1

4 to comment critically on the overall impact of a poem, showing how language and themes have been developed; Unit 1

Writing composition

Pupils should be taught:

10 to write a brief synopsis of a text, e.g. for back cover blurb; Unit 2

11 to write a brief helpful review tailored for real audiences; Unit 2

13 to write a sequence of poems linked by theme or form, e.g. a haiku calendar; Unit 1

Linked poems

Learning targets

On completion of this unit the children should be able to:

1 ➤➤ discuss how linked poems relate to one another by themes, format and repetition, e.g. cycle of poems about the seasons

2 ➤➤ comment critically on the overall impact of a poem, showing how language and themes have been developed

3 ➤➤ write a sequence of poems linked by theme or form, e.g. a haiku calendar.

Before you start

Background knowledge

Throughout the Learning Targets books at Key Stage 1 and 2, the children have encountered a wide variety of poetry. This unit allows them to investigate how poems can be linked by a common form and/or theme. They should be able to draw on their knowledge of rhyme, rhythm and poetic forms to contribute to class and group discussions; and produce poems of their own in draft and polished form.

All the poems in this unit are linked by the theme of weather. The activities in each session could be used with a selection of poetry centring on different themes, for example pets, wild animals, characters, etc.

Resources for Session 1

Copymaster 60 Shower
Copymaster 61 Rain

Resources for Session 2

Copymaster 62 Snow poems
A selection of poetry anthologies for group work

Resources for Session 3

Copymaster 63 Seasonal Haiku

Links to other units

Learning Targets: Fiction and Poetry Years 3 and 4
Year 4 Term 1 Unit 3: Poetry writing
Year 4 Term 3 Unit 3: Syllabic poetry
Learning Targets: Fiction and Poetry Years 5 and 6
Year 5 Term 2 Unit 2: Poetic forms

Assessment indicators

- Can the children read and discuss poetry in terms of thematic links?
- Can they identify poems that have the same poetic form?
- Can they produce their own poetry on related themes?
- Can they collaborate on the writing of a class poem?

Teaching the sessions

Session 1　①②③

Introduction　20min

 Give each child **Copymaster 60 Shower** and **Copymaster 61 Rain**. The children should read through the poems silently. Can they name the ways in which these poems are linked?

The children should see that they are linked by a common theme, i.e. rain and by a poetic form, i.e. shape poems.

Spend some time looking at the way each poet has written about the rain and how the content of the poems are reflected in the shape on the page.

Shower

- The layout of the words reflects the slanting appearance of heavy rain as it comes down.
- Each diagonal is in fact a traditional four line stanza with lines one and two rhyming and lines three and four rhyming.
- The poem begins with a fierce downpour of rain and ends with 'drops' as the rain stops.

Rain

- The layout of the words reflects the shape of a raindrop.
- It is not a rhyming poem.
- It begins by describing the effect of one drop and how, when combined, these drops become a 'moving green river'.

Allow the children to express their preference for one or other of the poems, supported by reasons.

Weather and shapes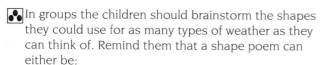

In groups the children should brainstorm the shapes they could use for as many types of weather as they can think of. Remind them that a shape poem can either be:

- where the words in the poem make the actual shape

or

- where the words in the poem follow the outline of a drawn shape or are inside the shape.

One child in the group can act as scribe and make notes like this:

Weather	Shape
cloudy	clouds
fog	long thin wisps

Summary

Record the children's suggestions on the board as a reference for their individual work.

My own shape poem

Each child should choose a type of weather and an appropriate shape and compose a shape weather poem. They should work in draft form, making lists of rhyming words, if appropriate, before they begin.

Look at the poem drafts and discuss with each child individually how their poem can be improved.

When the drafts are 'polished' the children should copy them neatly, using colours if appropriate, and the poems should be displayed.

Session 2 ① ② ③

Introduction

Give each child **Copymaster 62 Snow poems**. The children should read through the poems silently. Can they name the ways in which these poems are linked?

The children should see that they are linked by the theme of snow. The link through form is somewhat more difficult to identify, but both poems have no repeating verse pattern and an irregular rhyme scheme.

Spend some time looking at the way each poet has written about the snow and how the content of the

poems are reflected in the shape on the page. These are not 'shape' poems but the elongated verse form reflects the snow falling.

Snowy Morning

- Discuss the poet's use of the words 'bray', 'growls' and 'howls'. With what do the children normally associate these words?
- What effect does the snow have on the city?

If I Could Only Take Home A Snowflake

- What is the effect of the repetition of the first verse?
- With what does the poet compare the snowflakes? Why?
- Where do the children think 'home' might be?
- Why do they think the poet wants to take a snowflake to show his friends?

Finding a common theme

Give each group a selection of poetry anthologies. They should look for other snow poems, read them to one another and choose their favourite by majority vote.

Summary

Let each group read out their favourite snow poem and give reasons for why they chose it. These poems could be used as part of a display with the children's own snow poems.

My own snow poem

Each child should plan and write their own snow poem. They should work in draft form, making lists of rhyming words, if appropriate, before they begin.

Look at the poem drafts and discuss with each child individually how their poem can be improved.

When the drafts are 'polished' the children should copy them neatly, using colours if appropriate, and the poems should be displayed.

Session 3 ① ② ③

Introduction

This session will produce one or two collaborative poems, depending on whether there are four or eight groups.

Give the children **Copymaster 63 Seasonal Haiku** and read it through with them. Recap on haiku poetry (see Links to other units) to ensure the children are familiar with the form.

Discuss the children's reaction to the poem, leading them to see that each verse is a 'snapshot' of each season.

Haiku 30+ min

 Divide the class into four or eight groups. Each group (or pairs of groups) are going to produce a haiku about one of the seasons.

This activity can be adapted to various themes, e.g.

Cats
haiku 1 – cat sleeping
haiku 2 – cat hunting
haiku 3 – cat eating
haiku 4 – cat playing

As a starting point, the children should write words and phrases which immediately come to mind when they think of that season. From their list they should choose the most vivid images and work on the chosen words and phrases until they are in the right syllabic form. Stress that it is not necessary to have the season name in the poem, the descriptive words and phrases they use should make it clear which season they are writing about.

Be on hand to monitor the work in progress, especially as the syllable count might prove a stumbling block. Omitting or adding a definite or indefinite article or the 'ing' form of the verb are ways to tailor the lines to fit the required form.

Summary 10-20min

In the order of the seasons, one member of each group should read out their haiku to the class.

Discuss the finished cycle of haiku. Do the children think they give a good snapshot of the seasons and, put together, a good snapshot of the various types of weather throughout the year?

The haiku could be word processed in large coloured print and displayed.

fierce
  spring
    rain
     full
      gushing
       drain
drab   grey
 steely   puddled
  sky   street
   umbrellas Wellies
    held   for
     high   feet
cars   children
 make   want
  spray   out
   birds   harassed
    huddle   mothers
     away   shout
rain   cats
 becomes   lie
  drops   asleep
   slows   plants
    and   drinks
     stops   deep
    doors
     open
      wide
       people
       step
        outside

Moira Andrew

Rain

RAIN –
crystals melting
shivering a shape
at one with the wind
spitting angry thoughts in faces
creating a moving green river of the lawn
swelling the streams to cleanse
the polluted banks of debris
rainbow thumbprints
on grey tarmac –
RAIN

Kay Cornish

62 Snow poems

Snowy Morning

Wake
gently this morning
to a different day.
Listen.

There is no bray
of buses,
no brake growls,
no siren howls and
no horns
blow.
There is only
the silence
of a city
hushed
by snow.

Lilian Moore

If I Could Only Take Home a Snowflake

Snowflakes
like tiny
insects
drifting
down.

Without a hum
they come,
Without a hum
they go.

Snowflakes
like tiny
insects
drifting
down.

If only
I could take
one
home with me
to show
my friends
in the sun,
just for fun,
just for fun.

John Agard

Buds full, fat and green
Pink blossoms trembling on trees.
The warm breath of SPRING.

A burnished brass face
In an empty, cloudless sky
Smiles with SUMMER heat.

Curled and twisted leaves
Carpet red the cold dead earth.
AUTUMN'S withered hand.

Bitter winds of ice
Brittle grass like icy spikes.
Old soldier WINTER.

Richard Matthews

UNIT 2 | Book blurbs and reviews

Learning targets

On completion of this unit the children should be able to:

1 ➤➤ write a brief synopsis of a text, e.g. for back cover blurb
2 ➤➤ write a brief helpful review tailored for real audiences.

Before you start

Background knowledge

The children have written about books in terms of evaluation and personal response in earlier units. This unit gives them the opportunity to write about books for different purposes. Session 1 looks at book blurbs; investigates their structure and purpose, and provides models for the children's own writing. Session 2 introduces book reviews; comparing their purpose to that of blurbs, and provides models for the children's own writing.

Resources for Session 1

Copymaster 64 Book blurbs
Copymaster 65 Analysing book blurbs
Copymaster 66 Writing a book blurb

Resources for Session 2

Copymaster 67 Book reviews
Copymaster 68 Analysing book reviews
Copymaster 69 Writing a book review

Links to other units

Learning Targets: Fiction and Poetry Years 5 and 6
Year 5 Term 1 Unit 1: Evaluating novels and stories

Assessment indicators

- Can the children write about books, matching style and structure to purpose?

Teaching the sessions

Session 1 ①

Introduction | 15-20 min

▓ Begin by giving each child **Copymaster 64 Book blurbs**, which is a fairly typical example of a blurb. Part of the story is given to 'whet' the reader's appetite, questions are posed which will only be answered by reading the book, and an endorsement is given from a respected source. Use the blurb as the basis of a class discussion.

- Why do books have blurbs?
- What sort of information do they give to the reader?
- What information do they NOT give to the reader?
- Why do blurbs sometimes pose questions?
- Why do they sometimes include quotes about what others think of the book?

Analysing book blurbs | 20-25 min

⁑ This activity gives the children the opportunity to analyse book blurbs and to pinpoint common features. It can be approached in two ways.

1 Use **Copymaster 65 Analysing book blurbs**, so that all groups look at the same blurbs, making notes on what they have in common and how they are dissimilar.

2 Use actual book blurbs. Each group can have two or three fiction books to look at and then discuss which blurb they found most interesting and why.

Summary | 10 min

▓ A class discussion for activity 1 can be to compare the common features and differences which the children have found.

A class discussion for activity 2 can be for each group to talk about which book they most wanted to read, based on the persuasiveness of the blurb.

Writing a book blurb ⬚30 min⬚

👤 The children's individual writing work can be approached in two ways:

1 **Copymaster 66**. This gives random information about a book which can be used to write a book blurb when organised correctly.

2 Individual choice. Each child can choose a book they have recently read and write their own blurb without reference to the actual blurb on the back of the book.

In either case, if time allows, the children should be given the opportunity to word process their blurbs for a display. Encourage the children to lay out their work to look like a real book blurb.

Session 2 ②

Introduction ⬚20-25 min⬚

▦ Recap on the purpose of a book blurb and draw the children's attention to the fact that you can only read a blurb if you have the book in your hand.

Another way of finding out about books is to read book reviews. Ascertain what the children know about book reviews in a class discussion, ensuring the following points are covered:

• reviews are written by someone independent, i.e. by someone who has nothing to do with the writing, illustrating or publishing of the book

• they can be found in newspapers and magazines.

Once the children have grasped the first point, discuss how they think book reviews could differ from book blurbs, i.e. blurbs are a form of advertising to persuade you to buy the book, whereas reviews can say negative as well as positive things about a book.

Give each child **Copymaster 67 Book reviews** and discuss style and structure:

• fairly short

• usually one paragraph

• brief outline of plot without giving away ending

• reviewers' opinion on text and illustrations

• negative as well as positive reaction.

Analysing book reviews ⬚20-25 min⬚

♣ In groups the children can discuss **Copymaster 68 Analysing book reviews**. These are two more examples of reviews. The children should look closely at the language used to review Aesop's Funky Fables (it is quite sophisticated). They should also consider:

• who the books are suitable for

• whether the books are similar or very different

• which one they would be tempted to read based on the review.

Summary ⬚10 min⬚

▦ Compare the children's conclusions through class discussion and ask for their opinions as to the usefulness of book reviews:

• What purpose do they serve?

• What is the danger of only reading books that reviewers say are good?

Writing book reviews ⬚30 min⬚

👤 The children are required to write their own book reviews. They may choose to review a book which they have recently read or they can review an imaginary book. **Copymaster 69 Writing a book review** will support the children in this activity.

If time allows, let the children word process their reviews so that style and layout reflect the 'real thing'.

The Sighting

by Jan Mark

'One of my uncles or cousins,'
Dad said, 'saw things.'
'Did he really?' said Jack.
'Really see aliens?'

When Jack goes to his great-grandfather's funeral, he not only discovers a whole host of unknown relatives, but a real and vicious family feud. Something happened after the Second World War to split the family into fragments. But what? And can it really have anything to do with aliens?

'Jan Mark's witty, allusive style has a magic of its own for adolescents'
– *The Times Educational Supplement*

Cover illustration by Tom Connell

Puffin   ISBN 0-14-037865-0

Hurricane Horror

by Jack Dillon

YOUR LIFE HANGS BY
A THREAD AND TIME IS
RUNNING OUT. YOU'LL DO
ANYTHING TO …

SURVIVE!

A hurricane is heading towards Jason Mitchell's home and it is threatening to destroy everything. Most people are leaving town – but not *his* family. Jason's stubborn father is determined to ride out the biggest storm to hit the west coast in living memory. But at what cost?

Puffin   ISBN 0-14-038816-8

The Great Smile Robbery

and

Stinkers Ahoy!

by Roger McGough

The Stinkers – is there a gang more vile and horrible? No! That's why everybody loves to loathe them. And here are two of their funniest adventures – *The Great Smile Robbery* and its outrageous sequel, *Stinkers Ahoy!*

'Funny, inventive and rude'
– *Daily Telegraph*

'Don't eat when reading – you may choke laughing!'
– *Sunday Times*

Puffin   ISBN 0-14-130441-3

Writing a book blurb

Listed below are pieces of information which you can use in a book blurb about *The Lion, the Witch and the Wardrobe*. Can you sort it out and write a good blurb for the back of the book?

Book 2 in the Chronicles of Narnia

Lucy goes through the wardrobe into the magical world of Narnia.

'I couldn't put it down' – *The Book Reviewer*

Edmund is captured by the White Witch. Who is strong enough to defeat her?

It all started with a wardrobe.

When Lucy's brother Edmund goes through the wardrobe to Narnia, he is unlucky enough to meet the White Witch.

She meets the faun, and Aslan, the powerful Lion.

Aslan, the great Lion, must save Edmund. Will he succeed? And if he does, at what cost?

'A riveting read' – *Books for everyone*

Too Big!

Poor Neil Willis, everything in his life is too big. His school clothes, his favourite tree, his new cricket jumper – and now mum's wardrobe won't fit through the door. But no one listens to his protests until the perfect solution is found. Geraldine McCaughrean's **Too Big!** is a wonderfully chaotic tale, full of satisfying similes. Partnered by Peter Bailey's sharp drawings, this is a story children will love to read for themselves.

Too Big!

Geraldine McCaughrean

Corgi Press
£3.50

A Present for the Dog

Lynn Holly

Silver Press
£4.50

A Present for the Dog

The dog in question is a stuffed animal, much the worse for wear, which has been passed down from generation to generation in the Brown family. It now belongs to Katie, a six year old who likes everything neat and clean – including the dog! She embarks on trying to smarten it up with disastrous results! A clever story, let down by some poor illustrations and an abrupt ending.

Analysing book reviews

Aesop's fables are brought slap up-to-date in Vivian French and Korky Paul's vigorous retelling. *Aesop's Funky Fables* deftly weaves a bouncing text and frenzied artwork into a joyful collection which begs to be read aloud. The ten fables, written as prose or catchy rap-rhythms, combine old favourites – 'The Fox and the Crow' and 'The Hare and the Tortoise' – with lesser-known stories

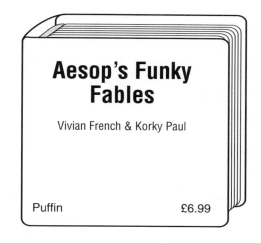

Aesop's Funky Fables

Vivian French & Korky Paul

Puffin   £6.99

– 'The Bat, the Bramble and the Cormorant' and 'The Traveller and the Bear'. Superb imagery, tautness of language and wordplay ensures loads of appeal and contemporary relevance. Styles are skilfully varied and instantly capture mood. Each story has its own rhythms – from the one-line verse of 'The Dog and the Bone' to the lyrical descriptions in 'The Boy who Cried Wolf'. The use of robust verbs and capital letters add extra verve and expression. Korky Paul's distinctive, scratchy illustrations, brimming with vitality, detail and humour, are the perfect match.

Thief in the Garden by Elizabeth Arnold tackles difficult issues with a light and humorous touch. Josh and Connor move with their mum to Grandad's house, who is unable to live alone any more. Grandad's mind is as muddled as his garden, and what's more, a mysterious thief has stolen the sausages. But an ancient cat gives Grandad a fresh interest in life, and when it dies, the story carries the reader gently along to the comforting ending. Ailie Busby's homely illustrations keep the reader smiling – and there will be plenty to discuss once the covers are closed.

Thief in the Garden

Elizabeth Arnold

Mammoth   £3.99

Writing a book review

Title: _____

Author: _____

Publisher: _____ Price: _____

Type of book: story ☐ poetry ☐ picture ☐

Use of book: adults to read to children ☐

children to read themselves ☐

Brief outline of contents: _____

_____

_____

_____

Illustrations: colour ☐ black and white ☐

excellent ☐ good ☐ poor ☐

What you liked about the book: _____

_____

_____

_____

_____

What you disliked about the book: _____

_____

_____

_____

_____

_____

Look carefully at the sets of pictures. Choose **one** set and write three poems, each based on one picture from the set. Each of your poems must have:

• the same number of lines
• the same rhyme scheme

1

      sunrise   noon   sunset

2

  wind beginning   strong wind   wind dying down
      to blow

3

     bud   flower   flower dying

Designing a book cover

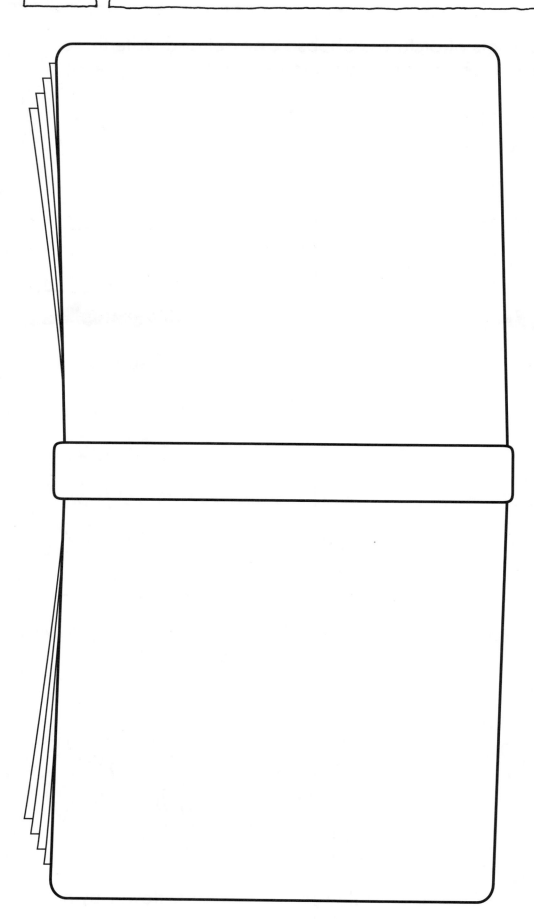

Use this copymaster to:

- design a front cover for a book. This can be fiction or non-fiction. Think of a title and author.

- write a blurb for your book. Make the blurb as interesting as possible so people will want to read the book. If it is a fiction book, don't give away the ending!

ACKNOWLEDGEMENTS

The author and publishers wish to thank the following for permission to use copyright material:

Moira Andrew for 'Shower', first published in *The First Lick of the Lolly*; ed. Moira Andrew, Macmillan Education (1986). Copyright © Moira Andrew.

Authors' Licensing & Collecting Society Ltd on behalf of the Estate of the author for 'Sir Smashum Uppe' by E V Rieu.

Wendy Cope for 'Kenneth'.

This publication contains material from the National Guidelines for Curriculum and Assessment in Scotland, English Language 5–14, produced by The Scottish Office Education Department. © Crown copyright. Reproduced with the permission of the Queen's printer for Scotland.

This publication contains material from the National Literacy Strategy, produced by the Department for Education and Employment. © Crown copyright. Reproduced under the terms of HMSO Guidance Note 8.

The Angel of the Central Line by Nina Bawden reproduced with permission of Curtis Brown Ltd, London, on behalf of the author. Copyright © Nina Bawden.

'The Vixen' by John Clare reproduced with permission of Curtis Brown Ltd, London, on behalf of Eric Robinson. Copyright © Eric Robinson 1984.

Andre Deutsch Ltd for 'Celery' by Ogden Nash from *Candy is Dandy: The Best of Ogden Nash*, 1994.

Doubleday, a division of Transworld Publishers, for an extract from *Timesnatch* by Robert Swindells, pp. 7-10. Copyright © Robert Swindells 1994.

Faber and Faber Ltd for an extract from *Clever Polly and the Stupid Wolf* by Catherine Storr, (1955).

HarperCollins Publishers Ltd for an extract from *The Phantom Tollbooth* by Norton Juster (1961).

A M Heath & Co. Ltd. on behalf of the author for an extract from *The Wolves of Willoughby Chase* by Joan Aiken. Copyright © Joan Aiken Enterprises Ltd.

David Higham Associates for an extract from 'The Centipede's Song' in *James and the Giant Peach* by Roald Dahl, Penguin Books (1961); and for an extract from 'Who's There?' (originally 'The Haunted Spacesuit') by Arthur C Clarke, first published in *This Week*.

Avalanche! by A Rutgers Van Der Loeff reproduced by permission of Hodder and Stoughton Limited.

Judy Martin Agency on behalf of Universal Pictures for material from *Apollo 13: The Junior Novelization*, adapted by Dina Anastasio, based on the book *Lost Moon* by Lovell and Kluger, Sapling, an imprint of Boxtree (1995) pp. 1–3.

Underground to Canada Copyright © 1973 by Barbara Smucker. Reprinted by permission of Irwin Publishing.

Spike Milligan Productions Ltd for 'A Thousand Hairy Savages' by Spike Milligan from *Silly Verse for Kids*.

Penguin Books Ltd for extracts from *Stig of the Dump* by Clive King, Puffin. Copyright © Clive King, 1963 and back cover copy from *The Sighting* by Jan Mark, Puffin (1999), *Survive: Hurricane Horror* by Jack Dillon, Puffin (1999) and *The Great Smile Robbery* and *Stinkers Ahoy* by Roger McGough, Puffin (1996).

'Jim' by Hilaire Belloc reprinted by permission of PFD on behalf of: The Estate of Hilaire Belloc. Copyright © The Estate of Hilaire Belloc.

Gervase Phinn for 'Seasonal Haiku' by Richard Matthews, included in *Lizard Over Ice*, ed. Gervase Phinn, Nelson.

The Random House Group Ltd for 'If I Could Only Take Home a Snowflake' by John Agard from *I Din Do Nuttin*, published by Bodley Head.

'Snowy Morning' by Lilian Moore from *Something New Begins* by Lilian Moore. Copyright © 1967, 1969, 1972, 1975, 1980, 1982 by Lilian Moore. Used by permission of Marian Reiner for the author.

Scholastic Ltd for reviews from *Junior Education*, June (1999).

The Society of Authors as the literary representative of the Estate of J. Meade Falkner.

Raglan Squire for 'There was an Indian' by Sir John Squire.

The Summer of Swans by Betsy Byars, copyright © 1970 by Betsy Byars. Used by permission of Viking Penguin, a division of Penguin Putnam Inc.

Virago Press for 'On Aging' by Maya Angelou from *Complete Collected Poems* by Maya Angelou.

A P Watt Ltd on behalf of the Literary Executors of the Estate of the author for extracts from *The War of the Worlds* by H G Wells.

Every effort has been made to trace the copyright holders but if any have been inadvertently overlooked the publishers will be pleased to make the necessary arrangements at the earliest possible opportunity.